HOW TO PREDICT
THE WEATHER WITH A
CUP OF COFFEE

HOW TO PREDICT
THE WEATHER WITH A
CUP OF COFFEE

AND OTHER TECHNIQUES FOR
SURVIVING THE 9-5 JUNGLE

MATTHEW COLE

The Reader's Digest Association, Inc.
New York, New York / Montreal

A READER'S DIGEST BOOK

First published in Great Britain in 2010 by Collins
HarperCollins Publishers
77–85 Fulham Palace Road
London W6 8JB

FOR READER'S DIGEST
U.S. Project Editor Siobhan Sullivan
Project Designer Jen Tokarski
Senior Art Director George McKeon
Executive Editor, Trade Publishing Dolores York
Associate Publisher, Trade Publishing Rosanne McManus
President and Publisher, Trade Publishing Harold Clarke

Library of Congress Cataloging-in-Publication Data
Cole, Matthew.
  How to predict the weather with a cup of coffee : and other techniques for surviving the
9-to-5 jungle / Matthew Cole.
     p. cm.
  Includes index.
   ISBN 978-1-60652-243-1 (pbk.)
1. Life skills--Humor. 2. Home economics--Humor. I. Title.
   HQ2037.C645 2011
   646.7--dc22
                                    2010051609

We are committed to both the quality of our products and the service we provide to our customers. We value your comments, so please feel free to contact us: The Reader's Digest Association, Inc., Adult Trade Publishing, 44 S. Broadway, White Plains, NY 10601

For more Reader's Digest products and information,
visit our website:www.rd.com (in the United States)

Certain activities in this book bring with them the possibility of injury, illness, loss, or embarrassment. But all adventure has an element of risk and it would be wrong to miss out on any of it, so please exercise common sense and take all necessary care when performing any of the activities included (and if you are a child under 16, always ask a grown-up for help). Rest assured that any risk arising from these activities is all yours. The author and publishers do not accept any responsibility for any harm that may occur from your decision to follow the instructions contained in this book.

Printed in The United States of America

1 3 5 7 9 10 8 6 4 2

Acknowledgments
With thanks to Mum, especially for recalling every detail of the M1 windscreen-wiper episode. Thanks to Denise Bates, Martin Toseland, and Helena Nicholls. Also to Jon "Leatherman" Riley, Ewen Thomson, and Lofty Wiseman, who all inspired bits of this book without knowing it. And finally, thanks to Joanna for lots of things, especially for her leniency over the smells from the car engine and any other mishaps (known or unknown).

CONTENTS

1. THE INDOOR BUSHMAN

2. TRAVEL WITH A SMALL "T"

3. THE HUMAN MULTI-TOOL

4. CITY ADVENTURES

5. WHEN DISASTER STRIKES

6. WORKPLACE STRATEGY

7. PURELY FOR PLEASURE

8. THE FUTURE

PREFACE

We were standing beneath an underpass to get out of the rain, and Dad came out with his favorite phrase: "We'll rig something up, son." I was about eight, I think. We were on a family trip to New York, and our windshield wipers had just broken. "We'll rig something up," he said, and that's what he did. Twenty minutes later we were back on the highway heading southbound with the wipers flip-flopping across the windshield. It's just that this time they were powered by a length of string fed into both back windows. My brother and I pulled as my sister called time.

As a feat of engineering, this wasn't much to shout about. But that's not the point. Some string and a few knots had changed our world. Out of a crisis, we'd conjured an adventure. We now had windshield wipers with voice-operated variable speed control, and it felt good. Dad was like a lot of dads back then; they had DIY in their DNA. They'd take car engines apart and collect miscellaneous odds and ends in empty jars (typically Araldite and string, batteries and radio parts, curtain hooks and electrical solder). Dad even had an extra-special premium selection in his bedside drawer, a shrine to his life's big purpose: fixing things.

There'd be no point in trying to emulate these old-fashioned, can-do dads today; they'd been schooled since childhood in improvisation and making do. If their bike wheels got punctured, they didn't use tire levers to ease the tires off the rims; they used spoons. My dad's puncture kit was three spoons wrapped in an oily rag, like a mechanic's wedding present. By the time they had kids of their own, these dads could wrestle a tire off a bicycle wheel with their bare hands. They were masters of the universe, lords of all physical forces, and they could fix anything, all before lunch, too.

When I became a dad I felt I should get a piece of the same kind of action. I dabbled a bit; I had my own collection of Ikea tools and kept a small screwdriver and a key for bleeding the radiators tucked away in my sock drawer. But this was small time. Really there's no way in the world I was going to spend a precious Saturday stripping down a carburetor or building a collection of washers that would fill several jars. It just wasn't me. So I found myself thinking back, rerunning my all-time favorite dad story. And looking again at what happened on that rainy highway, the answer struck me, like a piece of self-help from the days before airbags.

You see, although the wipers were working again, Dad hadn't

really fixed anything. He'd just sidestepped the problem. Armed with nothing but a ball of string, he showed the world who was boss. The message was clear: Make stuff happen, and if it happens to you first, then do something back. Oh, and keep a ball of string handy at all times.

Dad's rigged-up contraption had led me into the territory where simple always wins. In the digital age of downloads, here's a place where avoirdupois and analog still hold sway, where a father and son can reconnect to the big stuff that controls our universe. The tricks and schemes in this book are my personal doorway into this lost world.

Come and join me in the land where string is king.

THE PARABLE OF THE IPOD AND THE ONION

It was a huge viral video hit. People couldn't get enough. It showed you how a guy had charged his iPod by sticking the USB charger in an onion left overnight in some Gatorade. That's fascinating, I thought. So did thousands of others. It seemed brilliant. It was a huge hit. Most views of the week. Hey everyone! You can charge your iPod with a vegetable! Onions 1, Apple Inc. 0.

But something didn't add up. It doesn't work. Initially this is disappointing news. But what really matters is the groundswell of glee that greeted the very idea. Gatorade contains "electrolytes," so it had a ring of credibility. Sticking a USB connector into an onion, though? Do you really think so? 'Course not. Yet, logic aside, tens of thousands of people were prepared to believe.

What this reveals is a longing for an elemental simplicity to deliver us from all of life's frustrating, tedious annoyances. We want simple truth to triumph over the modern world's incomprehensible complexity. This book offers some suggestions as to how it can. Only none of the suggestions involve an onion; sorry. . .

INTRODUCTION

Warning! This is a guide to survival in the real world. That's the world you see when you step out of the elevator at Ikea. It's not a place where Swiss Army knives, compasses, or the rubbing together of sticks are particularly appropriate. And the eating of bugs and leaves would be just...stupid.

Whatever you've been told, our ancestors didn't develop their skills of survival so that they could stay alive in the woods. They had other plans. They wanted to move into a city and buy a car with a GPS.

How to Predict the Weather with a Cup of Coffee celebrates what happens once they got there and man's primal instincts came to town. It revives some of the tricks from our primitive past and unleashes our flair for survival on a nasty new threat: the tedium of modern life. I see this as a shot of red-blooded purpose into our pale urban backsides, turning the 9–5 into a nonstop adventure.

Some of the tricks and schemes in these pages are stolen from the Neolithic hunter; some are purloined from the notebook of the Victorian explorer and some you already do every day. I call it "urban bushcraft," and it's an art and a science that's been in development ever since we had Neanderthals for neighbors. A lot has happened since then, so here's a quick recap.

OK, this is how it goes. First there is this ape. He walks out of the forest, gets into some basic grooming and the result, eventually, is you. You're the slickest life-form to wear a loincloth and you can turn your hand to anything. With your super-sized brain and those freaky opposable thumbs, you know what you want, and you know how to get it.

You fast-forward seven or eight millennia of breakneck progress, plus a few more when (frankly) you're just coasting. You rise above every challenge you face with boundless ingenuity. You get better and better at everything, and as a result you have less and less to do. Forget this hunting business; let's start a farm. Fed up with building shelters? Let's get into property development. These buttons are a bit awkward. What about a zipper?

And suddenly, you've cracked it. Survival is in the bag—shrink-wrapped, bar-coded, and scanned. Bleep! Do you need any help packing today, sir?

Now, just hold it there a second. This part is important. Don't worry, you've got a moment while you swipe your card.

Think back a few thousand years. You've just tracked your first antelope and you're standing there, spear cocked, all ready to turn it into lunch. Imagine how that felt. Now look at yourself. Instead of a blood-splattered spear and a steaming great antelope, you've got a PIN number and a bag full of groceries. Different isn't it?

What you may have just experienced as you compressed ten thousand years of human experience into one supermarket second is "the niggle." It's that little larva of doubt worming around the back of your mind. Welcome to the modern world; this is what it's like, I'm afraid. In theory things are great, all urges are satisfied, and all needs are met. But there's something missing: excitement. Oh, that reminds me—don't forget to buy yourself a lotto ticket.

HARDWIRED AS CAVEMEN

When our brains were hardwired, the job description was just one word: survive. Back then, life was in the balance every day. Sundays and holidays included.

But times changed and so did the priorities. We used to have to know when to hunt and when to run away, but now we just need to know which day to put the recycling bins out. We're programmed for cut and thrust, a 24/7 existence that's contested tooth and claw, not a 9–5 workday with occasional coffee breaks.

Of course, all this lying around not doing much is great, in theory. The problem is "the niggle." This is worth going into, because if nothing else, it explains why you get such a kick out of lighting the barbecue.

Our primal urges, you'd think, cover a pretty straightforward shopping list: hunger, shelter, warmth...done. But there's one more thing evolution has armed us with. It's the urge to feel the thrill that comes with satisfying all the other urges. That rush of bringing home the bacon is a reward in itself. In the 1960s, psychologists would have called that a biofeedback loop. To you and me it's a vicious cycle and, because of it, we're completely hooked.

Our DNA tells us to look for the kicks we got from all the big, bad dangerous stuff that we just don't have to do any more. And now, like a dog chasing rabbits in its sleep, we can't stop. As you stand at the barbecue and smell the fat sizzling on the charcoal, you're acting out your favorite flashback. Man make fire! Cook, eat... yum! And you can't switch this stuff off. It took a few million years to develop this baby. Get used to it, it's yours to keep.

If your life is spent going undercover behind enemy lines or hunting grizzlies from a log cabin beside the Yukon, this may not apply. Life may be exciting enough. But for the rest of us, there's "the niggle." No wonder we get a bit cranky from time to time.

THE KEYS TO THE FERRARI

Over the centuries we've gotten very good at keeping our caveman brains quiet by throwing them a bone now and then. It's what the entertainment industry has been doing for centuries. Movies are fantasy workouts for the primal self. They fall into two camps.

First there's what I call the "Back to Eden" fantasy. This is the one where the primitive self gets to go back home and lead a simple life, just as nature intended...It's *Huckleberry Finn, Robinson Crusoe, The Waltons, Survivor,* and *Lost.* This is powerful stuff. Has anyone ever watched *The Jungle Book* and actually wanted our man-cub Mowgli to go back and live in the "man village"?

The other kind of daydream for the caveman inside us all is the Tarzan fantasy, where the savage gate-crashes the modern world. It's why *Basic Instinct* was the best ever title for a movie, and why shoot-em-up games take over the male mind. It's all chewing gum for our instinctive self, which explains that odd sense of calm that comes over you as you walk out of a slasher movie. Chase scenes do the same job, too; deep down we recognize how it feels to be the prey, whether playing chase in the playground or being hunted down by a robotic Terminator for the tenth time on DVD. It gives us the chance to rehearse it all again. And inside we squeal with pleasure.

Now we come to the fun part. It's like discovering a Ferrari sitting in your garage. Or if you're not that into cars, it's where you find out you have a secret talent for wiggling your ears...whichever you prefer.

Your instinctive self is a highly tuned and finely calibrated piece of evolutionary engineering, but for most of the week you just leave it in the garage. We're compelled to keep this powerful machine a secret from the civilized world. The urge comes over us in two ways:

1. We think if we give in to instinct, we'll start turning up at meetings with wild staring eyes and stains on our shirts. So we just don't talk about it; we pretend it's not there. It's the 800-pound gorilla in the room.

2. We treat instinct like a hyperactive dog. It can be kept locked inside as long as you give it a run in the evenings and on weekends, whether by going to a horror movie, going to a shooting range, or reading a Tom Clancy novel.

How to Light a fire

Bushcraft **Survival**

But of all the occasional outings for our instinct, one type stands out head and shoulders above the rest, loud and proud in khaki shorts, hiking boots, and obligatory fleece. Yes, it's time to throw out the deodorant and head for the woods to learn about survival skills. Under the watchful gaze of men with long knives and a faraway look in their eyes, you get to skin rabbits and distill your pee into drinking water.

For millions of men, this stuff is an outlet for pent-up frustrations; it's a secret ventilation shaft from the soul through which the inner caveman gets to emerge into the outside world. And of course, it's insurance against the collapse of global civilization, when the ability to track hedgehogs and signal in semaphore would be quite handy.

But what if the closest you come to a desert in your day-to-day life is a square mile with no cash machine, and the highest summit you've seen today is the top of your office building? Why escape to a fantasy wilderness to get our primal rocks off? Why not use all our innate brilliance to generate some red-blooded adventures right here in the 9–5, where it matters most?

It's time for bushcraft to come out of the woods. It's just as much fun, far more relevant, and there's no vague whiff of urine.

Man loves to make a good fire. But why persist with sticks and stones when you can use a car battery and a Brillo pad with far more impressive results?

Navigation used to be about reading the stars and finding the campsite. For the urban bushman, it's about finding where on Earth you parked the car.

And here's the best part. Urban bushcraft doesn't mean turning your back on the comfort of central heating, wireless broadband, and a fridge full of cold drinks.

There's a lot to learn. Let's get started.

BUSHCRAFT BASICS

Bushcraft. You've heard the term a lot already, but what is it, really? It's a way of describing the know-how and tricks that enable you to make life a lot more comfortable outdoors. The great thing, of course, is that we only gave it a name once we didn't need it that much anymore. It's cool stuff for campers who don't like things too easy.

We started to become fascinated with "bushcraft" as a leisure interest after World War II, when it offered some simple certainty in an uncertain world. Ellsworth Jaeger of the Buffalo Museum of Science was one of the great collectors of what he called Wildwood Wisdom, writing it all down and keeping the spirit alive.

Back then, in the United States and Australia especially, people hankered for times gone by on the wild frontier, when a man would cook up his coffee on the embers at night, and his best friends were his coonskin hat and his gun. The appeal lived on, and it survives today, when there's a Starbucks on every corner and a man's only friend is the Bluetooth-enabled device in his pocket.

Though times have changed, there's a constant theme from the Bushmen of the past to the modern day urban bushman. Both of them are happy and relaxed in their chosen habitat. They're getting good at living here, and they like it that way. It's a nice place to be.

Bushcraft can be easily confused with that other stuff on TV shows where former Special Forces guys show you how to bake a skunk or get out of quicksand. For these boys there's a very different attitude. They just want to get the hell home. It can get confusing to tell one from the other at times, so here's a simple identification guide to help.

BUSHCRAFT	SURVIVAL
TROUSERS	
Shorts. (The shorter the shorts, the more likely they are to be Australian.)	Cargo pants. Gore Tex and camouflage gear
CONDUCT	
Combed hair, Boy Scout appearance. Happy to be in the woods.	Breathless, unshaven. Desperate to get home, quick
LIGHTING A FIRE	
Natural methods using friction such as bow drills	Gasoline from the wreck of a car is preferred
SOURCE MATERIAL	
Ancient wisdom and tribes	Special Forces such as Navy Seals

1.
THE INDOOR BUSHMAN

Most survival guides would leave you politely at your front step, on the presumption that if you're home, then you're safe. But for us indoors is where it all begins. The reason is simple: The urban bushman is driven to unearth new challenges and new thrills in the most familiar of places, and, for that, there's no place like home.

With this fresh perspective and a few new tricks, your humble abode will be transformed into the Great Indoors—a place that screams adventure, with its wide expanse of carpet, and seductive lineup of gadgets (just look at all those remote controls!), not to mention the benefit of central heating and more coffee than you could ever drink.

It falls naturally into two sections. To begin, this chapter concentrates on handy skills to turn everyday annoyances at home into a journey of discovery; telemarketers, household chores, and arguments over the phone are all problems we're out to solve.

But there's another important dimension to bushcraft with your slippers on, far beyond pure practicalities. Home is a place of respite from the need for results that muscles in on the rest of your life. So in the second part of this chapter, you'll find some bushcraft for the weekend, where we take things at a more leisurely pace. There are discoveries to share with the family and suggestions to ensure you'll always have something to do when it's raining.

SCREENING CALLS WITH A MICROWAVE

If you've ever felt that your cell phone rules your life, this one's for you; a guaranteed way to dodge unwanted calls.

HOW TO SCREEN YOUR CALLS WITH A MICROWAVE

This stems from one big difference between two gadgets that use microwaves. In order to communicate, the cell phone gets microwaves to shoot around, passing through anything in the way, whether it's solid brick or gooey gray matter. Our microwaves, on the other hand, prefer to contain the waves and focus them on a single bowl of soup. The microwave stops them from escaping with a Faraday cage (a mesh in which the holes are too small for microwaves to squeeze through).

So when your phone rings and you suspect it's someone you'd rather avoid, here's what to do:

1. Start to move toward the microwave (switched off).

2. Answer cheerfully, "Hello . . ."

3. Gradually move your phone in and out of the oven and watch the signal strength fall and rise. With the phone held in the oven (keep the oven switched off, of course), you lose contact completely. Just inside the open door, it fades in and out.

4. Now assume a confused voice: "Sorry I'm losing you, we're going through a tunnel" . . . etc.

The strength of this system is that it can be used after you've answered—far more convincing than hanging up mid-call. After a couple of tries, you'll become a virtuoso, bringing the caller in and out of range at will, playing him like a fish on a hook; then, just as he thinks he has gotten you back . . . you're gone for good. (This also works with a wireless landline phone, though it's harder to get away with.)

Remember not to shut the door completely—that dinging sound is a dead giveaway.

THE TOP FIVE ITEMS REGULARLY MICROWAVED IN THE NAME OF ENTERTAINMENT

First the microwave brought us the TV dinner, then it made it possible for generations of boys to blow up Ping-Pong balls and experiment on M&Ms. Now the two have converged to such a degree that there are people sitting down with frozen dinners to watch a cable show devoted to putting everyday objects inside a microwave.

1. Ping-Pong ball	*the original and the best explosion*
2. Soap	*a volcano of lather solidifying into a surreal sculpture*
3. CDs	*a circular light storm*
4. Twinkies	*the creamy middle wildly oozes out of the cake*
5. M&Ms/marshmallows/grapes	*more gooey pyrotechnics*

CALLING ALL MICROWAVES

If I said that you can cook popcorn with the signal from your cell phone, would you believe me? Not strong enough? Then how about with ten cell phones? If the idea seems to make sense, it's because of an assumption that follows from the knowledge that cell phones communicate using microwaves. The very word conjures up images of frozen dinners, doors that go ping, and a lot of 1970s science about cooking from the inside. But today's communication microwaves (the ones that allow you to share ringtones with your Facebook friends in Kuala Lumpur) aren't the same as the microwaves in the microwave oven (the ones that heat a lasagna in one minute). You can't cook with cell phones any more than you can phone someone via the defrost setting.

MICROWAVE SAFETY TEST WITH A CELL PHONE

You need a cell phone, a microwave, and another phone (a landline will do fine). Check that your cell has a signal, place it in the microwave, shut the door, and call it up. You should find you go straight to voicemail, because the microwaves can't reach the phone. If it rings, it means the microwaves can get in and that means you've got problems, because if the waves can get in, they can get out as well. Watch out for your eyes. It stings when they start to cook.

THE FREEZER FIGHTS BACK

Compared to the microwave, the fridge and the freezer are the old timers in your kitchen, still running on technology barely changed since the 1940s. Of all your appliances, these oldies, humming quietly to themselves, are barely noticed. So it's especially pleasing to be able to help them get one over on new technology.

"The click of death" is the name sci-fi–obsessed tekkies give the sound a computer's hard drive makes when it can't retrieve any data, and it usually means that it's time to panic. On hearing it, your palms go clammy, the blood drains from your head, and when people ask, "Did you save it anywhere else?" you have to fight the temptation to scream. In all cases of panic, the advice is always do something, anything; make a cup of coffee, dig a hole, bake some bread. Well, I'd suggest what you do is put your hard drive in the freezer; it will keep you busy and it might just help.

WARNING! This is a last resort that may not work. I offer it to you in the knowledge that it's helped many people before, and that right now you'll try anything.

ANOTHER WARNING!! This can get quite technical, but the urban bushman isn't one to shirk the challenge of reading an instruction manual or downloading a help page or two.

Day one

- Remove your hard drive. (If you don't know how, you'll find instructions easily enough online. Look for them before you start pulling your computer apart.)
- If you can, fit a USB connector into the drive (unless you're an IT champion, you'll need help . . . which means more web surfing). This just helps you to hook up your drive very quickly, but it's not essential.
- Vacuum seal it in a plastic bag as best you can.
- Leave it in the freezer for a few days (this isn't a precise science, some people find a few hours is long enough).

A few days later

When the big day comes, be prepared to retrieve as much of the data as you can very quickly (freezing is only ever a temporary fix).

Here's how to do it:

- Take your drive out of the freezer. If you wired a USB connector into the computer, plug it in. Otherwise reinstall in the usual way. Use an ice pack or freezer block to keep it cool.
- Start to search for the drive and open the media. Muttering "C'mon, c'mon" usually helps here, too.
- If the click of death is replaced by the ping of hope, don't start to celebrate until you've transferred everything to another disk. Start with the most essential stuff first.
- All copied? Now you can celebrate!

How it works

When you kick the television, it's because you know just enough to think that it might help; if it does, though, you haven't got the faintest idea why. This is a bit like that; I see it as old-fashioned physics administering a gentle slap to a technological young upstart.

There are two plausible theories as to what's going on:

1. **The mechanical theory:** It could be that the "read" head of the drive is jammed, and that freezing makes the metal parts shrink just enough to free it for a few minutes.
2. **The magnetic theory:** Hard drives store information magnetically, and the magnetic field gets stronger as the recording media get colder, allowing the drive to read it more easily.

Oh, and before you shut the freezer, you may as well get out a frozen lasagna . . . it's time for dinner.

DISHWASHER COOKING

This is perfect if you can't face doing any cleaning up after you've cooked. The longest cycle on the dishwasher (usually 90 minutes or so) will cook fish and vegetarian foods perfectly well, while you process a load of dishes at the same time.

The dishwasher chef's primary skill is wrapping up each dish in a watertight little parcel of foil. The key here is to make sure the foil is tightly sealed so no water can get in and ruin your food.

POACHED, STEAMED, AND GLEAMING SALMON STEAKS

There's no limit on space (unless, of course, you already have a fairly full machine), so go for broke with some big meaty salmon steaks.

Serves four

Cooking time: 70 minutes

Ingredients:

- Four large salmon steaks
- Seasoning
- Tinfoil

Steps:

1. Season each steak and wrap with dill and lemon inside a foil package with tightly crimped edges. If you're using detergent in the wash cycle, consider sealing the salmon inside a freezer bag.

2. Place the packages on the top shelf and set dishwasher to its highest and longest setting. A 1-inch (2–3 cm)-thick steak will cook to pink perfection in a 70-minute hot cycle.

DISHWASHER LASAGNA

Serves four

Cooking time: 1 hour

Ingredients:

Use a recipe of your choice for vegetarian ricotta or spinach lasagna.

Steps:

1. Make the lasagna in the middle of a large sheet of foil, building up layers of pasta and filling as you go.
2. Wrap lasagna securely in the foil.
3. Place the package flat on the bottom rack of the dishwasher.
4. Set to the normal wash cycle and repeat if necessary until cooking time is reached.
5. Before serving, let the lasagna stand for five minutes.

VET YOUR FRIENDS WITH A PET

WHAT YOU NEED: a perceptive pet (dog, cat, horse)

Consider the coyote on the prairie and the dachshund on the couch. Both are on a constant vigil—alert to the faintest sound or the slightest whiff on the breeze. Wild-wolf genes and razor-sharp senses have made them the perfect four-legged early warning systems.

Trackers and wilderness people know all of this and study animal behavior to pick up all kinds of information that they'd otherwise miss. An urban bushman can get in on this same action by putting his pets to the same use. Here are some rewarding applications of pet instincts that can make your social life a whole lot simpler.

This isn't as crazy as it sounds. Wild animals need to read the behavior of others for their own survival. If a stranger comes onto their patch, they need to read its intentions fast. They tell the strong from weak and friend from foe, and they do it by being experts in nonverbal signals.

Working in your favor here is a quirk of modern life. Domesticated over many generations, your pet considers itself part of your human pack / flock / family. And so they need to be as expert in reading human body language as they once were at reading their own species. Then, once they have spotted something, the information is then passed on to others in the pack. That means you.

Pets, just look at them; all they do is watch people all day. It's no wonder they're good at this. Have a go at these tests, and you may find the result surprising.

THE PET LIE DETECTOR

This is perfect for fans of the Lassie films. ("Look! He's trying to tell us something!")
It's common enough for an owner to claim that his pet senses when he's in a bad mood, when something's up, or when he's stressed. This last one is especially interesting. Stress is exactly what a lie detector picks up, too. If pets can spot stress in humans, and then communicate it to us, we're in business. Next time someone's lying or getting stressed in your company, look at how your pet behaves and make a note of the signs. Now you're ready.

Here's how it works:

1. Get someone to tell a huge whopper of a lie in front of your pet. They may need to elaborate and go into great depth.

2. Look at how the pet reacts. Is your dog or cat trying to tell you something?

Okay, so this all depends on how well you can read your furry friend. But this is something you can practice. Just like a polygraph (lie detector), it's all in how you interpret the evidence. Once you think the communication is going well, you can try a more scientific test.

Set up a scenario where a succession of people enters a room to talk to your pet. Some of them will tell a pack of lies, others will tell the truth.

Meanwhile you sit with headphones on, unable to hear them. You can only look at your pet. Make notes of which one was which, purely from the animal's response.

Legal note: This kind of lie detector evidence is not admissible in court.

THE PET PERSONALITY TEST

Are you hanging out with the wrong crowd? It's never easy deciding whether or not someone is on the level, or just a waste of time. But your pet can help.

Perfect for:

Settling arguments ("I told you I never liked him!")

Every pet owner knows that their animals take to some people and not others. Dogs pick up right away if a visitor is nervous around dogs. And don't cats always go straight to the right lap for a nap? But it goes deeper than that.

As the leader of the pack, you are the person your pet needs to tell about any threat. Pets see it as their job to let us know their doubts about anyone coming into our territory.

We've already covered how to read the signs your pet puts out if something's not quite right. And you can tell if your pets are either aggressive or friendly toward a stranger. So now's the time to start taking note of their responses to the strangers you bring home. It's hard to deal with too many shades of gray here. We're making broad judgments on someone's character, so be bold.

When you have a little database of ten or so, look through them and see if there's a pattern emerging. You'll never look at your friends in the same way again.

THE WEEKEND BUSHMAN

Now that your chores are done, it's time to focus on something more edifying: bushcraft that soothes the soul, especially designed to fill up your weekend or while away an evening in or a morning off.

I'll start with a favorite demonstration of the mood-altering possibilities of bushcraft in the home.

HOW TO TURN YOUR TV INTO A COSMIC TIME MACHINE

This is a cure for a condition commonly known as "Nothing on TV." When we complain that "nothing's on," what we mean is that there's nothing that's going to grab us by the scruff of the neck, slap us on both cheeks, and demand our attention. Well if that's the case, then this will fix it.

Here's how to use your TV to pick up a 13.7 billion-year-old signal from outer space, in three easy steps.

1. Turn on TV.
2. Unplug satellite or cable box.
3. Stare at static.

That "snow" or static is background "noise" generated by the soup of radio waves washing around the Earth. When you're tuned to *The Simpsons*, the signal is so strong you don't see the noise. But when the TV has nothing else to latch on to, it tries to translate the "noise" into a picture, and "snow" or "static" is the result. Now turn up the sound and listen, because here comes the good part. Most of this static is caused by the radio and TV signals that are constantly buzzing around the world, Chinese minicabs, Somali weathermen, and Russian tank commanders. During the Battle of the Atlantic in World War II, a young telegraphist on a Royal Navy cruiser picked up what he thought was a coded signal from a nearby German U-boat. Out there in the Atlantic, they tended to think about U-boats a lot. Nobody could understand the message or even recognize the code. The report was duly sent back to experts, who couldn't understand how this message had come to be received in the mid-Atlantic. It wasn't any code or language they recognized. Then, eventually, its origin was tracked down. It was a short-range transmission from a Russian tank commander in Stalingrad, appearing as bright as you like thousands of miles away at sea. This is a shining example of the erratic behavior of radio waves and their tendency to pop up all over the place, a syndrome known as analogous propagation.

But 1 percent of the noise that you're seeing (and hearing) is something else; it's the radiation left over from the event that gave birth to the entire universe, it's the receding echo of the Big Bang, now showing on your very own TV.

I'll pause here while you take in the enormity of what you're looking at. Now stare at the screen again. One percent of that fizzing energy and activity is coming to you from something that happened more than 13 billion years ago.

For me this is a bit like smelling salts: You can use it to snap you out of any mood, at any time. And that's not the end of it; the explanation of how we know all this is pretty good, too.

How it works

If we'd always had digital TVs, we'd never have seen this phenomenon. But in the old days of analog, TV had to pick up a wide range of frequencies, and this microwave echo of the Big Bang—gradually fading as it spreads through our ever-expanding universe—

just happens to overlap into the same range, so our TVs were able to see it. Its proper name is Cosmic Background Radiation (CBR). It's on the radio, too, somewhere in all that white noise between stations.

CBR was found by a pair of American physicists in the 1960s. They were trying to listen to the stars and were getting increasingly irritated by a constant noise on their powerful receiver. At first they thought it might have been caused by pigeon poo on their dish, but they had it cleaned and it was no different. Then they wondered if it could be radiation from nearby New York, but they pointed their dish the other way and it was still there. Eventually they found it wasn't even coming from within the galaxy but was present everywhere throughout the universe. Then they looked at each other and realized what it must be. They had found what was left of the heat from the Big Bang.

SOFA SCIENCE LESSON

Whenever kids complain there's nothing on, then, seize the chance to grab their attention by turning the TV into a cosmic data receiver. Relating it to *Star Wars* in some way might help, too, depending on the demographics. But get it in while you can; before long all TVs will have built-in digital tuners, and it will be much harder to tune into the cosmos by just tuning out.

FORECAST STORMS WITH A TV SET

All over the world television is turning over to digital signals. But the laws of science have no plans to follow suit, so there is still a use for your old analog TV—tune it in to the weather.

This works because electrical storms emit radio waves. To pick up the weather, you need to be able to tune in to the lower ends of the VHF (Very High Frequency) band. At the first sign of thunder, get ready to catch a spectacular lightning storm on TV at around 55 MHz. Try Channel 2. It really helps if you turn the brightness right down until you can't see a picture. When lightning strikes nearby, it throws horizontal bands of light across the previously dark screen. As the storm gets closer, the bands get bigger.

How it works

Lighting causes interference by generating signals on a similar frequency to Channel 2. And when the storm's less than 10 miles away, the signal is strong enough to completely illuminate the screen.

THE TV TWISTER DETECTOR

With more spectacular weather comes a more spectacular display on the TV. This is a bone fide method of tornado tracking, and we owe it all to the heroic work of Newton Weller of Des Moines, Iowa, who discovered it in 1968. This was after years of study and accumulating 100 old TV sets in his garage.

The whole thing works because tornadoes give out their own

signal, and this was Weller's big discovery. If you want to know, they are blueish purple flashes emitted high in the thunderhead at about 18,000 feet up. And they just happen to be on a similar frequency to Channel 2.

First tune into a regular channel, say 17, and turn the brightness right down low until you barely see a picture. Now switch over to Channel 2. It should still look dark. If you see flashes, then the Weller Method is telling you something.

If your set does suddenly brighten for more than a few seconds at around this frequency, and you can't see any lightning, then there could be a twister coming. If the screen goes white, the twister is closer than 5 miles away.

THE TRUTH ABOUT THE REMOTE CONTROL

A visitor from Mars would know immediately that the TV remote control is important to us; why else would we appear so bereft whenever it's out of our sight? It's our equivalent of the speaking stick that they pass around in mud huts when somebody wants to talk, except ,of course, the remote is usually a sign to shut up. But it's an honor to hold it, a symbol of power and control.

REMOTE CONTROL FREAK

The beam from the remote control is invisible to humans, and as a result the people you share your TV with prefer not to think about how it works, writing it off as a piece of magic. But really it's infrared light, which is light from a part of the spectrum we can't see, and because it's light, it can bounce off mirrors (which shouldn't surprise anyone, but it still does). This all makes for a good way to retain control over your living room.

Just configure a system of mirrors so you have a direct line of sight to the TV from the kitchen/dining room/study. Point the remote at the image of the TV and zap as normal. The rule is: If you can see it, you can zap it. It's especially handy if the kids are watching in one room and you're cooking fish sticks in another.

This technique for channel changing is especially recommended for pool players.

ZAPPER HOKUM

Like all important icons in our lives, the remote control is often the subject of half-truths and outright lies. One claim I've seen too much of recently is the suggestion that you can make an emergency replacement with a flashlight and a plastic lens. Don't believe it, no matter how convincing the website or video clip may appear. The remote works by sending a digital signature with encoded commands, far too complex to be copied by a flash of light. And here's a technique for keeping it in your grasp wherever you are in the house.

CARPET STEALTH

Whether you're avoiding waking the children, avoiding detection after a night out, or avoiding the in-laws, there are times when the ability to creep around the house without making a sound is a precious thing.

This is where you need your slippers. They are to you as the soft-soled moccasin was to the Seminole Native American, the expert trackers of the American woodland. By adapting the wisdom of the Seminole, we turn creeping downstairs into an exercise in primitive stealth. Using his feet to feel the way, that noble hunter could creep across the forest floor in total silence, creating a picture of every twig and rock underfoot. If this is too hard with slippers, try it with socks* and pick your path between the Lego pieces and those electronic toys ready to go off at the merest touch.

SIX GOLDEN RULES OF CARPET STALKING

1. **SLIPPERS:** Use them to feel the way.
2. **HEEL FIRST:** On carpet always bring the heel down first.
3. **FEET STRAIGHT:** On carpet, to avoid a giveaway "rip" as your foot brushes against the pile of the carpet, it's vital that your feet are straight so that the big toe points the way.

---

* Slippers are quieter so what you lose in touch, you may gain in stealth.

4. **EDGES:** Avoid creaky floorboards by treading on edges near the wall, especially on staircases and bare floors.

5. **ATTIRE:** Remove noisy clothing to avoid "trouser swish." Corduroy is a favored fabric for hunters because it's relatively quiet.

6. **SWITCH OFF:** Don't fret, just believe you won't be heard. The leopard doesn't have self-doubt as it stalks its prey; nor should you.

To avoid squeaks when opening a door, dab some cooking oil on the hinge with a tissue. It does its work in seconds. To be doubly sure, apply upward pressure as you turn the handle.

A note on carpets: The shorter and tighter the weave, the noisier the carpet. Shag pile is preferred for stalking in slippers. On natural flooring, go for socks; never stalk in bare feet (unless powdered) in case they stick.

THE INDOOR FORAGER

Watching a TV survival expert eating bugs and berries in the wilderness can make you feel like you're missing out. One solution would be to head for the Amazon to root around for edible leaves and medicinal shrubs. But don't bother; there's more than enough in the potted plants and vases around the house, and this way you can fit your foraging into a commercial break. But do consult your flower guide (pages 42–43) first, to be certain you know which plants are definitely edible and which plants aren't.

HOUSEPLANTS AND FLOWERS—IDENTIFICATION GUIDE FOR THE INDOOR FORAGER

Use the guide on pages 44–45 to identify some common indoor edible plants. Always give the plants a good wash before eating and follow the guidelines closely. If you're in any doubt, don't eat it.

THE YUCCA—A ONE-STOP ACTIVITY CENTER

It's one of the most common plants in the indoor environment. You've been watering it all these years; now it's time for some payback.

You can eat it, make rope and blankets with it, weave baskets and carve figurines, and it's the best wood bar none for lighting fires, so it's not surprising that Native American tribes mythologized the powers of the yucca. If you are prepared to sacrifice part of the root and trunk, you have a day of yucca fun ahead, rounded off nicely with this evening's fire-lighting ceremony.

Uses
YUCCA CHOPSTICKS

Time: one hour

The smooth wood is perfect to eat from, and it splits easily. Start with a branch that looks about the right size to get one or two pairs of chopsticks from it and split it down the middle. Whittle away until one end of each is rounded, leaving the other end in its raw twiglike state for rustic authenticity.

SPIDER PLANT

CHRYSANTHEMUM

SPIDER PLANT (LATIN NAME CHLOROPHYTUM)

Habitat: Usually found in hanging baskets or in a student's bedroom.

Edible uses: All of the plant is safe to eat, and the tender plantlets that shoot off the main stem are especially good in a stir-fry.

Medicinal use: In India it's commonly eaten as a leaf vegetable, but the real interest is in the root, thought to have a medicinal use as a natural Viagra.

CHRYSANTHEMUM

Habitat: Supermarket flower buckets, funeral bouquets.

Edible uses: The flowers and seeds are edible, and the leaves make a tasty tea. The variety called chop-suey greens *(Chrysanthemum coronarium spatiosum)* is especially good and rich in vitamins; eat young shoots cooked or raw and leaves raw in a salad. The flower petals, blanched quickly in boiling water, are a decorative addition to salads.

ALOE VERA   **CHINESE LANTERN**   **MIXED BOUQUET**

ALOE VERA

Habitat: Designer apartments, doctors' offices.

You can eat parts of some varieties but this strictly applies to only certain varieties.

Medicinal use: A handy first-aid kit, especially good for soothing little burns, cuts, and scrapes. Just make a slit down a leaf, and rub the gel over the affected area.

CHINESE LANTERN

Habitat: Grandma's windowsill.

Edible uses: If you have a sweet tooth, these are for you. The flower is good raw or cooked, on its own or as part of a salad. The longer the flower is open, the sweeter it gets.

MIXED BOUQUETS

Habitat: Anywhere on Valentine's Day or Mother's Day.

Edible uses: Petals help any dish, so root around in a mixed bouquet for your favorites. Rose petals are especially palatable, a sprinkling of carnations makes a peppery addition to any meal, and tulips have a fresh taste, a bit like cucumber.

YUCCA BRUSHES

Time: two hours

You need to have prepared for this by soaking some leaves in water for a couple of weeks. Now pound the leaves with a stone to get rid of the green pulp until just the fibers are left. Tie a bunch of fibers close to one end. The Navajo would bind one end tight for use as a hairbrush; the other looser end served as a clothes brush. Or, if you prefer, wind the fibers to make string, rope, baskets, or a blanket (maybe just a very small one).

YUCCA FLOWER FRITTER

Time: 30 minutes

To do the least damage to your plant, just eat the flower petals; they're good raw but best lightly cooked (dusted in flour and fried in oil for five minutes). If your yucca has a fruit, you're in for a juicy treat. The stem of the flower is edible, too, best if peeled and boiled like asparagus. All to be eaten with the yucca chopsticks, of course.

YUCCA SOAP

Time: 40 minutes

Take a bit of the root and crush it in a bowl of water until it starts to get sudsy. The more you work at it, the more lather you get. Now you're ready for the Navajo hair wash, all the rage in the spas of New Mexico.

THE POWER-ASSISTED YUCCA FIRE CEREMONY

In general starting a fire by rubbing sticks is far too much work.

With some dried yucca, however, you have the best chance

you're going to get of pulling it off, which has a certain satisfaction of its own. You can match the TV expert without leaving the living room.

It all comes down to the yucca's uniquely low ignition temperature.

To experience the thrill, without the sweat, here's what you'll need:

- dried yucca wood (after harvesting, leave for a week somewhere dry and warm)
- a power drill with blunt drill tip
- a ball of tinder, shredded paper/wool

Carve a small bowl-shaped dent into your yucca* and drill down into this until it begins to smoke. You need a blunt drill so that you don't bore through the soft wood too quickly.

Once the friction creates enough heat for the yucca wood to start smoking—you'll see it and smell it at the same time—keep going a little longer. Now whip the drill away and look for a tiny red-hot lump—or a piece of "coal." Very quickly, tip your piece of coal into the tinder ball, blowing on it gently in the way you've seen on all those survival shows.

If you don't succeed at first, keep trying. Or use a match.

Now put up a few shelves—you may as well, now that you've gotten the drill out.

---

* The bowl is to help stop the drill from slipping.

THE CEILING SUNDIAL

The ceiling sundial brings the intrigue of the celestial cycle, of solstices and seasons, into your bedroom, and it's a pretty good way to tell if you're late for work as well.

Lying in bed one morning looking at the lines of sunlight thrown across the ceiling by reflections from the car windshield below, I invented the ceiling sundial. I really did, even though Sir Isaac Newton had done the same. 350 years earlier. Whether it's the father of modern physics, you, or I, it's pretty obvious that an ability to tell the time by looking at your bedroom ceiling is a thing worth having.

All you need is a mirror positioned on your window ledge so that a spot of light is thrown onto your ceiling. This is the simplest form of sundial; it requires the least amount of equipment, it's fast to set up, and best of all, the space available on the ceiling allows for a bigger dial, giving extreme accuracy.

Note this only works if you have a south-facing bedroom, or at least a view of the southern sky from your room (anywhere between SW and SE facing is perfect).

As well as a south-facing room and available ceiling you will need:

- a small mirror
- glue or tape
- a pencil
- a clock

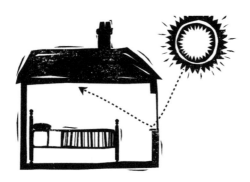

FIXING THE MIRROR

In the morning, fix the mirror to the windowsill (or a sash halfway up) so that it reflects a spot of light onto the ceiling. Position the mirror horizontally, as high (close to the ceiling) as you can get it.* Now follow the progress of the spot and mark its position every hour with a pencil. Well done, you now have your very own spot dial, or at least the makings of one. The dial part (the equivalent of the clock face) takes a bit longer.

How it works

Before deciding how to mark your dial on the ceiling, you need a basic grasp of how a sundial works. I'll cover it in three points.

1. Everything the sun does outside is the inverse of what happens on the ceiling. As it moves across from east to west, the reflected beam moves across the ceiling west to

---

* Position mirror close to the ceiling; otherwise, the dial's range is magnified over a much wider area and won't fit on the ceiling.

east. The lower the sun is in the sky, the farther into your room the beam is projected.

2. The route of the spot changes daily, sweeping across the ceiling between two extremes: the winter and summer solstices. In the middle of these extremes is the equinox; that's the moment every March 21st and September 22nd when the sun follows the same course in the sky and the days are exactly the same length as the nights. Mark out your dial on a date that's as close to the equinox as possible; this will help you position the equinox line (the midpoint of your dial) close to the middle of the ceiling.

3. The hours fall within flared bands that radiate from a center point somewhere outside your window.

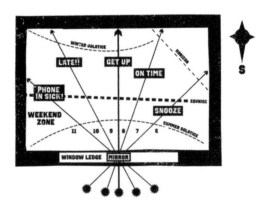

THE DIAL

Now you're ready to mark your dial. Start the whole process in the morning, close to the time you want the dial to be most effective.

Look at the time and position the mirror so that it throws a spot on the ceiling wherever you think best, remembering that you need to be able to see the time easily when lying in bed. Leave space for the hours you'd like to come before and after.

Diehard sundial fans mark a central "meridian"—the line the sun crosses at midday. But that's way too late. I prefer to make 9 o'clock the center of things. By restricting the range to the vital few hours of the morning, your dial can be more accurate, and you don't need such a big ceiling.

THE OFFICIAL LINE OF LATENESS

Mark the hours with stickers or pencil crosses (you still need your clock at this point). Before you begin to mark in your hour lines, you need some of the year to pass. Mark the same time at the equinox and one of the solstices (or any two days a few months apart) and draw straight lines between them. Once you have these hour lines in place, the dial starts to take shape. I use masking tape first before committing to paint, allowing me to tweak the lines later for supreme accuracy.

I'd start by marking only the hour by which you have to be out of bed, making the simplest, clearest dial of all: a new meridian— the official line of lateness.

THE BEDROOM SHRINE

Five thousand years ago the inhabitants of the Orkney Islands built Maeshowe, a stone chamber expertly aligned so that on the winter solstice the setting sun sends a shaft of light along the entry passage to hit the back wall where the bones of the ancient elders were buried. Going to see it is a pretty good way to enthuse children with the whole idea of the celestial calendar. Or you could just show them the Indiana Jones movie that uses the same idea. Either way, you need to know that you can adapt the windowsill mirror trick to make your own bedroom version of this sacred shrine.

Here's how:
- Pick your significant date (say a birthday).
- Through careful positioning of the mirror, mark a suitable spot where the celestial beam will hit the wall.
- Now position your chosen icon (football poster, cartoon character, trophy) so that at sunrise or sunset on the given day, it is kissed by the golden rays that peep over the horizon. You will need to provide the soundtrack yourself.

Alternate suggestion: I often use the sunspot as a random CD-selection technique. But as a seasonal touch, you could arrange things so that at 10:00 A.M. on December 25th a sunbeam illuminates the Phil Spector Christmas CD on the shelf, in preparation for its annual outing.

URBAN BUSHCRAFT THROUGH THE AGES:
THE MAN WHO INVENTED BAKED ALASKA

To round off our indoor exploration, here's an account of what can happen when a great inventor turns his mind to the home. His name was Benjamin Thompson, and he had to leave home in a hurry after backing the losing side in the Revolutionary War. He spent the rest of his life in Europe picking up wives and mixing with royalty while pursuing his career as a scientist.

What I love about Benjamin is this: His curiosity as an inventor was totally uninhibited by the view that science should be all about grand schemes for the progress of mankind. Instead he was fascinated by daily life in the home, and he made it his focus. As his writings show, he knew this uniquely domesticated approach singled him out. "It is really astonishing how little attention is paid to things near us and which are familiar to us... How few persons are there who ever took the trouble to bestow a thought on the subject in question (the familiar) though it is in the highest degree, curious and interesting," he wrote.

His area of expertise was heat and everything associated with it. But while others were thinking about steam engines and spinning machines for textiles, he fixed his efforts on the home. It strikes me that he was a gadget guy, way ahead of his time. He revolutionized the fireplace and did the same for the oven. Then he repeated the feat by designing the first modern coffee percolator. But he wasn't yet done. In noticing the low heat conductivity of the egg white, he gave the world the greatest application of his domestic genius: Baked Alaska.*

Now Leonardo da Vinci is reputed to be the most creative inventor of them all. But even he never dreamed of putting ice cream inside a baked dessert!

---

* The only blemish on Thompson's record is that he didn't call it Baked Alaska, but Omelette Surprise.

2.
TRAVEL WITH
A SMALL "T"

"Hi there! So, which way did you come? Was it the freeway or did you take the turnpike?"

I don't think I've ever arrived at the end of a long drive and not found myself part of this little men-only ritual: the conversation about the route I took to get there. I've been a keen student of this one for a few years. Both men are reciting a script they know by heart, slotting the pieces into a puzzle that celebrates an obsession with how we got here. I always want to go for a little high five at the end, but that hasn't quite caught on yet.

I mention this because it helps identify what this section is all about: travel with a small "t." The urban bushman isn't interested in capital "T" travel—with trips of a lifetime; he's focused on being home by bedtime.

Travel doesn't have to have an exotic destination to broaden the mind. Simply bringing the spirit of the great explorers to the daily commute turns it from lost time into a heroic endeavor. And it's in that spirit that we learn how to navigate by satellite dish or use a highway trip to cook chicken wings on the car engine. Whatever our chosen mode of travel, we're moving on in the name of science and of adventure.

DRIVING BY NUMBERS

If you're a guy, I'm sure you want to know how to get one up on the other guy in the inevitable conversation about directions you have whenever you arrive any place by car. A little bit of study now can equip you with a battery of road numbering knowledge that will make you ready for anything.

This works best over long distances, so you get to show off your knowledge of the two-road numbering grids. That's right, grids. Oh, you didn't know? I'm sorry. Let me run you through it right now.

U.S. TWO-DIGIT ROUTES

This is a simple grid where odd numbers run north to south and even numbers run west to east. The way I remember this is to picture the figure 1 (an odd number) and visualize it as a pointer running top to bottom (North to South). You'll soon get it.

But because these things are never as simple as they seem, you need to remember that U.S. Route 101 is still seen as a two-digit route, with 10 being considered as one digit.

The rest of it is pretty logical with numbers running 1–101 from east to west (as you'd write them from left to right) and 2–98 from north to south (as you'd write from top to bottom).

Interstate Highways

The numbers of interstate highways follow a system that's the opposite of the two-digit routes, with numbers getting bigger from east to west (right to left) and from south to north (bottom to top). It helps keep identically numbered routes apart.

CARS: BUSHMAN BEHIND THE WHEEL

I know that cars are useful, and I do understand that they arouse deep passions in people, but let's not pretend that man and motor are made for each other. Don't get me wrong, the potential is tremendous, but the practicalities are a problem.

The car is a symbol of freedom, yet we spend about an hour a week trying to find a parking space. We dream about 0–60 mph in five seconds, but most of the time we're outpaced by pedestrians. We love the privacy, but all we do in a traffic jam is pick our nose and adjust the mirrors.

The best way I can sum up our relationship with cars is this: Man had the ingenuity and brilliance to invent the car, and yet whenever he wants to go for a drive, he can never find his keys. And that's just frustrating. So it falls to the urban bushman to close some of the gaps that have opened up between men and cars and discover new ways for us and them to get along.

THE REAL HIGHWAY CODE

Humans evolved over thousands of years, while cars have been around for just a few decades. It's clear when you think about it that the person in the driver's seat is a man first and a driver second. This is the simple secret behind the vocabulary of signs and signals that are the real Highway Code.

All mechanical means to communicate with another driver are flawed. A flash of headlights meant as a friendly invitation to pull over can be seen as a hostile shot across the bow, and the horn is just as bad. We have no evolutionary experience with cars, and so we end up judging them on completely flawed criteria, seeing them as if they were people, finding an angry expression in the headlights or a nasty word in a perfectly innocent license plate.

The key is simply this: Forget the car and make contact with the driver. In anonymous isolation behind the wheel, he's free to assert his baser instincts and probably will. But adding a social dimension (however fleeting) changes all that for good. This explains why drivers with the roof down are much less likely to misbehave—we can see them.

The ultimate deterrent to aggressive driving is eye contact. Cyclists and pedestrians instinctively know how to use the human eye as the ultimate traffic signal, and they do it all the time. Once they make eye contact, they know that the driver's seen them. But that's not all. Eye contact has a deep primal meaning. It's a signal that we're no longer dealing with a ton of metal moving at speed but with another human, and that changes the rules considerably.

Eye contact

The change in our behavior when you take away eye contact shows its deep significance. It's so important that we've developed an almost supernatural ability; when somebody looks us in the eye, even at a distance, in an instant, we know. There are a couple of things that stop this from happening: dark glasses and most significantly of all, traveling at over 20 mph.

GALTON'S CODE FOR ADVENTURE

I really like Sir Francis. This man would never compromise, and there's a lot to learn from his approach. In fact I've distilled the essence of his outlook for the bullet-point generation. After all, no urban adventurer is fully equipped before they're acquainted with Galton's Code.

Galton's Code

- Nothing is too trivial for reinvention by the adventurer.
- Maintain standards of dress at all times.
- Use tools you can trust; shun new-fangled gadgets.
- It's what you find out that matters, not how flashy your kit is.

FINDING PARKED CARS THE NATIVE AMERICAN WAY

Every evening millions of us park our cars on the street where we live. No wonder, then, it's so hard to find a space out there, and we have to drive miles to get a spot. The end result is that we wake

Urban Bushcraft through the ages: Sir Francis Galton

To a Brit like me, the nineteenth-century explorer is the equivalent of the pioneer of the Old West. These were the people whose heroic endeavors and horrific blunders shaped our world. They were men from the days when a man was a man and a moustache came as standard.

Sir Francis Galton was an explorer who saw travel as an art and a science. For Sir Francis, exploration wasn't about having the right kit and looking good in a bandanna; it was the noble endeavor of a civilized mind. When traveling in Africa, he took with him theodolites, writing desks, and ink stands. He always packed a dinner jacket, insistent that dress code wouldn't slip just because he was in the tropics. He had an especially gory version of the money belt. It involved stashing an emergency gemstone by cutting yourself, placing it under your skin, and allowing the skin to seal it in as it healed.

But the thing I like best of all is his work on the art of rolling up sleeves. Like all of us Sir Francis knew that when we roll up our sleeves, there's every chance that in a minute or two they'll roll back down again. And that's fairly inconvenient when sewing gemstones into one's own arm. Sir Francis was not the sort to tolerate this so instead, he determined to fix sleeve-rolling for good and started to rethink the whole procedure. After some experimentation he made a breakthrough that is a gem of Victorian blue-sky thinking and a gift to us all from the great age of exploration and discovery.

"When you have occasion to tuck up your shirt sleeves, recollect that the way of doing so is not to begin by turning the cuffs inside out, but outside in. The sleeves must be rolled up inwards towards the arm and not the reverse way. In the one case the sleeves will remain tucked up for hours; in the other they become loose every five minutes." (Francis Galton, The Art of Travel, 1855)

In his book Sir Francis gives sleeve-rolling as much space as all the obvious explorer stuff (how to cross a river with a mule, the correct way to approach a native, etc). That's why I love him. He knew that fixing all the small stuff improves life just as much as fixing the big pieces.

up every morning and wonder where the heck we left the car last night. The standard response to the problem is to defend your parking space with a scaffolding plank across two chairs. But for the urban bushman, it's a chance to hone a craft borrowed from Native Americans. And it's less likely to provoke a war with the neighbors.

It depends on learning a system of "blazes." These are the secret trail signs Native Americans used to show others the way—blazing the trail. In this adaptation for the urban reservation, the trail leads discreetly to your parked car. If you pass this on to friends and family, you can share the location of the car day or night. There's no need to ask where it is; just follow the blazes.

Blazes are useful whenever parking in a large parking lot or parking on the street every day for work. For lazier days another popular method is to take a picture of the car (and space number) on your camera phone.

MAKING BLAZES

There are a couple of choices. You can use chalk or some kind of marker (such as tape) to record your trail, or make blazes out of stuff lying around like gravel, grass, litter, or twigs. This organic approach is more satisfying. But the benefit of using chalk or tape is that it's far easier to spot (for the initiated) and can be especially useful when leaving a trail for somebody else to follow.

Native American blazes conformed to a simple grammar; you just need to adapt them for your native landscape, using bits of urban detritus.

To make a blaze with found items:

Twig blazes

Rock blazes: A crisp packet or scrap of litter under the bottom rock helps the blaze to stand out.

Marked blazes

Marked on street signs, road signs, or each street corner, these blazes create your own coded directions, legible to the initiated only. It's graffiti's grown-up brother.

Once you've mastered this, you can get a bit more communicative:

KEEP GOING, NEXT RIGHT, and KEEP GOING, NEXT LEFT

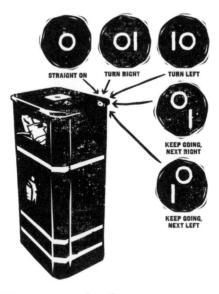

Blazes: graffiti's grown-up brother

WHY MEN LOVE GIVING DIRECTIONS

There aren't many things that the human male enjoys giving to total strangers, but directions are one of them. We all know the sense of swelling pride when someone asks you to direct them: It's so strong that when you see a person poring over a street map, you even get an urge to offer to help. Anyone who really needs assistance—a struggling person with a heavy suitcase, for example, or with small children—can forget it, but when it comes to directions, we love to show we know.

Conversely, we hate asking for directions; it's a sign of weakness, showing that we don't know. Being given directions is so repellent that it's almost impossible to listen. We've all done it, and we've all seen it happen. You're giving out directions and you can see by the look in the other person's eyes that it's just not sinking in. He was with you up to the second piece of information (turn left just after the gas station . . . or was it just before?). But from then on, forget it. He's nodding politely but, inside, he's put his fingers in his ears while shouting "not listening, not listening!" He just can't help it.

BLAZE THE TRAIL TO YOUR HOUSE

Instead of rubbing up against the male ego in a rather unpleasant way, share a primeval tracking opportunity next time you need to direct a visitor to your house. By laying a few simple blaze trails from the big obvious start points, you can challenge anyone to spot the trail to your door. It's a test of your carefully laid blazes, the person in question gets to use his knack for following a trail, and nobody has to listen to any instructions; it's a win-win situation.

HEY, WHERE'S MY CELL PHONE?

Who remembers the days before cell phones? Those were the days when all you had to check your pockets for before you left the house was your wallet, keys, and a dime for the phone. What did you do when you were running late or you missed the train? What about when your friends weren't where they said they'd meet you? These days you just give them a call. Maybe send a text. But back then, what did you do? What were the routines and the systems we all fell back on when things didn't go according to plan?

It's a question people have been asking since around 1995. What did we do before we had cell phones? The answer is that we did fine, but we've just forgotten how.* We don't know how we managed without these things because existence without them is unthinkable. We've assimilated the capabilities of that tiny communications computer in our pocket and remodeled life around it. And although the human brain never forgets physical skills like riding a bike, it seems that conventions of behavior can disappear overnight.

It's been the same old story for a long time now. From the wheel to the iPad, mankind invents stuff, then forgets how to get along without it. Generations of culture and learning are put to one side, never to be found again. It's just the way we are. We're gifted inventors and very quick learners, but oh so easily distracted. Our minds are capable of inventing an automobile but completely unable to find the keys.

Urban bushcraft is our attempt to swim against this stream of forgetting and to remember that as we progress in some ways, we may also regress in others. We're surprised to learn that there are moments in history when we knew more than we know now. Take the Pantheon in Rome and its huge concrete dome. For centuries engineers couldn't understand how it was built. Two thousand years after its construction, we are still guessing. It's constructed

---

* Here's what we did. We showed up on time; we made a plan, and we stuck to it.

from a type of concrete that outperforms the stuff we use today. It really shouldn't be standing. But go and see it. It is.

I often like to imagine what you'd learn if the clock went into reverse. You'd remember how to meet a friend without calling him every few minutes. Then maybe you'd find out how to hitch a horse and cart or to navigate by the stars, and I like to think that my handwriting would certainly improve.

CAR-ENGINE COOKING

Don't say, "Are we there yet?" Just ask, "Is it done yet?"
Using the heat of your engine to cook while you drive is a classic of improvisational brilliance, adding value to every gallon of fuel by delivering a piping hot meal on arrival at your chosen destination. But economics and convenience are only the start of under-the-hood cuisine's attraction. It's an extension of our love affair with the car itself; it represents a man's freedom and is something he can get completely obsessive about.

The principle of wrapping your food in foil and sticking it on a hot engine is simple, and many a good meal has been had by putting a hot dog somewhere snug under the hood, clocking up 40 miles or so, and tucking in. But that's the equivalent of a Boy Scout chucking a foil-wrapped potato into a bonfire. The joy is in the refining: Each foray sharpens the appreciation of the special relationship among the three variables; travel time, mileage, and choice of dish.

Instead of oven temperature and cooking time, recipes give mileage and speed. For instance, at 65 mph shrimp cook in about

50 miles, chicken wings need about 130 miles, and a full roast dinner is done in 300 miles.

The relationship among the three variables in engine cooking is echoed in several car makers' logos. The three-pronged star of the Mercedes symbol is an especially handy reminder.

50-MILE HOT DOG

There's a lot to learn before you can safely cook a proper meal on your engine, but experience is a great teacher. Next time you're due to take a 50- or 60-mile drive, turn it into a field trip and launch your career as a car-engine chef.

Wrap a couple of hot dogs in foil (tightly) and find somewhere to wedge or jam them snugly on top of the engine. Keep them away from moving parts and make sure they're held in position when the hood is down.

Pack a couple of buns (plus ketchup/mustard) and some oven gloves (they're what the glove compartment is really for), and drive off. On arrival, check out the hot dogs for heat; if hot, drive in and enjoy your first car-cooked meal. If the hot dogs are still cool, realize it just takes practice, and read on.

CAR COOKING KIT

- Oven gloves
- Tongs (for access to especially tight spots)
- Hot dogs
- Mustard/relish
- Herbs/spices
- Spare tinfoil
- Notebook for recipes and observations

WHEN TO COOK WITH THE CAR

- Camping trips: You've arrived, it's raining, and you have to put the tent up. Thank heavens for piping hot burgers and crispy french fries.
- Dinner party (you're a guest): Offer to arrive with something hot to bring straight to the table—a guaranteed talking point.
- Dinner party (you're the host): Assign each guest to bring a different course, based on how far each has to travel.
- Fishing trips: Enjoy the catch of the day at its freshest, after a twenty-minute drive to a secluded picnic spot.

GETTING STARTED—THE TWO TESTS

The cardinal rule of engine-block* cooking is to work with the "configuration" of your car—its individual engine anatomy. Two basic tests can help you look at what's beneath the hood with the eye of the chef** to discover the best parts for quick cooking (hottest), for slower cooking (coolest), and the shape and size of all the nooks and crannies where you can slot in some food.

Test 1: The heat test

Time: ten minutes

Take your car for a five-minute drive to get it warm, park, and lift the hood. Hold your hand over various parts of the engine to see how hot they are. Be extremely careful—as the aim is to feel the heat WITHOUT getting burned.

If you wish, you can integrate this test with the 50-mile hot dog, and use your spare hot dog as a thermometer. If it sizzles, you've hit somewhere hot.

---

* The engine block is the main chunk of the engine in the middle. It has fuel injectors and spark plugs (with cables attached) sticking into it. This is where the power and heat come from.

** Expert car-engine cooks take pride in having different recipes for different cars, which gives an idea of how different each car can be.

Remember that you're looking for a range of spots with different temperatures so that you'll be able to cook two very different dishes at the same time. Ignore plastic parts—they won't get hot.

Usually, the hottest part of the engine will be the exhaust manifold (the big iron tube running the length of the engine from front to back with two, four, or six other tubes from the engine joining it). On older cars, the top of the engine block can be a good place, too. As you go, keep an eye out for any likely crevices or crannies where you could fit a foil-wrapped package of food. If you have a natural dip or indentation on top of the engine block, and it's hot, you're off to a good start.

Test 2: The foil crunch test

Time: ten minutes

Now that you have an idea of where you might be able to cook on the engine, you need to find out what you can fit into it, and where.

Make a loose ball of foil and put it on any likely spots on top of the engine. Through trial and error find the clearance of the space by seeing how much the ball is crushed when you close the hood. Be precise, so that the hood will hold the food packages snugly in position.

Use the same principle to find out the size of each of the cooking cavities. Now when you cook, you'll know where each item will fit best. Bulk up smaller items to the right size with extra foil.

ENGINE ENVY

Now that you're paying attention to what's beneath the hood, everyone's car can become a source of interest. The next time someone lifts the hood on their flashy V8 engine, have a look and drool, not at the thought of the power it generates but at the delights that could be so effortlessly cooked in that deep V-shaped indentation along the top of the engine block.

The Jaguar E-type is considered the prime example of this unique feature of the V8, and chefs have been known to fit enough fillet steak or rib eye to cook for six people with ease.

THE HIGHWAY COOKING CODE

- Cook anything you'd cook in the oven, but avoid sloppy casseroles and stews (vibrations will spill juice everywhere).
- Triple wrap everything you cook in foil.
- Fit your food to the spaces available; overwrap to fill the space.
- Safety first! Only put food in and take it out with the engine off.
- Never place food near the line that joins the accelerator pedal to the engine or any of the air intakes.
- Don't pull any wires or force a package to fit where it won't.
- Always use tongs or oven gloves to remove hot food.

THE CAR-B-Q

Cooking on the move has a rich heritage that connects medieval horsemen of Asia with American truckers of the 1950s. For both, it was a ritual that defined their nomadic way of life; one group put raw steak under their saddle to give it a pounding in preparation for a victory feast,* the others heated hot dogs on their exhaust manifolds to provide a lazy snack.

The car-b-q recaptures that spirit of romantic adventure. It's food designed to be eaten outdoors. As the smell of your mixed kebabs and steak wafts through the grille, you can catch the eye of the driver in the outside lane knowing that you're the real king of the road around here.

How to car-b-q:

1. Plan your travel time and select your meat and fish course to suit (see cooking guidelines in steps 2–4).
2. Follow precooking or marinade directions from any conventional recipe. Think about catering for the ravenous nomad inside you. Which will it be: the Mongolian horseman or the American truck driver?
3. Wrap the food in a variety of package sizes to fit the available slots and secure them in place.
4. Unwrap it and serve.

To spice it up, why not add a few side dishes such as stuffed peppers, flat breads, or sliced eggplant to accompany your meat, fitting them in where you can. Vegetable dishes can go into the cooler spots of the engine.

---

* The horsemen in question were the Tartar warriors of Siberia, and from them we get the name Steak Tartare.

HARMFUL FUMES

A well-maintained engine won't emit foul or harmful by-products; they're all channeled into the exhaust. If you can smell your food cooking, that's good news, because it means you'd also smell any nasty gases coming off your engine. If you can smell something nasty, you need to get it checked urgently, whether you're cooking or not.

What's that smell?

One last word of warning, in the form of a confession. Last summer, my family began to comment on a dreadful smell in or around our car. I thought it would go away, and they'd soon stop complaining. But, it didn't. Then a week or so later the terrible truth dawned on me. It was coming from under the engine, near the manifold. It could only be one thing—a lost piece of jerk chicken from a cooking foray at least a month earlier.

Removing it was an hour-long operation (in the end I had to use an extendable umbrella handle). And it took a couple of days to get the smell out of my nose, and longer to get over the dented pride that came with such a schoolboy mistake. This is the first time my beloved family will learn the truth (if they read this far). The lesson from all this is to be strictly organized with all food placed on your engine. Leave nothing behind—count each item, and then count each again.

> **Chris Maynard and Bill Scheller** introduced the world to gourmet engine cuisine in the 1980s with their book *Manifold Destiny*, which includes recipes such as Hyundai Halibut with Fennel, Poached Fish Pontiac, and Cruise Control Tenderloin.

BACKSEAT CHEFS

All the campfire classics for kids will work well on a car engine. The foil-wrapped banana (unpeeled) with chocolate stuffed inside through small slits in the skin is, of course, a classic. On a hot engine allow 30 miles to achieve gooey bliss. Baked apples need about 50 miles.

NEED A BOTTLE OPENER?

Most car-door mechanisms have a handy built-in bottle opener on the doorframe. Look for the D-shaped loop of metal that keeps the door shut.

WINDSHIELD BAKERY

This is great for keeping kids amused on a camping trip. You use the car, but you don't even have to turn it on. Just make sure it's in the sun. Make some cookie dough or pancake mix, put it on a baking tray, then leave it exposed to the sun inside a closed car for 2–3 hours, and return to pick them up in time for lunch.

On a sunny day, when temperatures can reach almost 90°F (30°C), a car's dashboard can heat up to around 200°F (90°C), which is perfect for baking cookies.

THE BUSHMAN AT THE BUS STOP/COMMUTING

Cavemen commuted, too; it's something we've always needed to do. And with 10,000 years or so of experience, we should be able to negotiate it without breaking a sweat. By drawing on the wisdom of great commuters of the past, the urban bushman takes the angst out of the daily trip to work and turns it into a twice-daily break.

TWO STEPS TO A CALM COMMUTE

Step 1: The 60-minute rule

An hour of travel a day feels civilized. With two half-hour journeys, the brain has time to acclimatize and to assimilate. But it's more than just a feeling that tells us this is right; it's a commuting instinct that's as deeply pre-programmed into our primitive brain as the need for a good night's sleep.

Man is a territorial animal and likes to patrol his patch. The bigger the patch, the better; that way he gets more food, more friends, more of everything. But he's a cave animal as well, and so he wants to finish his day curled up in the familiar comfort of the family home. Now you see how commuting was born.

This intrigued physicist Cesare Marchetti. Wanting to know more, he pulled together a ton of research to show how long people spend each day in routine travel, whether from an African village or a Japanese city. He found it was all stunningly uniform; in all societies there's a tendency to spend a total of 1.1 hours a day in transit.

Then he went on to show that this figure, "Marchetti's Constant," hasn't changed throughout history. As evidence, he found that the size of Greek villages and ancient cities like Rome, Marrakesh, and Persepolis, and even his native Venice, are all of a size that you can walk from the outskirts to the center in about half an hour. And as transport modes developed, from the horse and cart to the Austin 7, the city limits were pushed back.

Marchetti showed that 90 percent of our total travel time is spent inside this 30-minute zone, and we have every reason to think it's always been that way. So if your commute is feeling more stressful than it should, recalibrate. If it's under an hour there and back, stretch it out. And if it's running over, consider drastic action to hit the target time. Man has favored a 30-minute each-way commute throughout his history, and that's some serious conditioning. You'd be a fool to fight it.

Step 2: The commute as a break

The Star Trek "teleporter" always seemed like a good idea, getting beamed to wherever you want to be in a second. But hang on a minute; look at what you'd miss out on.

Traveling puts you in a bubble, protected from outside annoyance and irritations. The French philosopher Michel de Certeau called journeys like this an "incarceration-vacation," and I know what he meant. You're captive, all you can do is sit there—and that's a huge relief.

Next time you're on a regular journey by bus or by train, allow yourself to revel in the serene isolation. Look out of the window, switch off, and ask if life could be any better. Even the phone can't break the spell: Reception is in and out, and you can hardly discuss the new marketing strategy in front of the whole bus. Commuting is a break from the mania for productivity that fills the rest of your life. It's "me-time," and it comes free with your ticket.

BUS SEATS AND HOW TO GET THEM

If the urban bushman is a sniper picking off the problems of daily life, then the daily struggle for a seat on a rush-hour bus or subway makes perfect target practice.

Go through your mental checklist:

- Is it part of your daily routine? Check!
- Is it stressing you out? Check!!
- Can we find a strategy to overcome it that's deeply satisfying? Check!!!
- Its fate is sealed: time for this nasty little threat to be neutralized.

If you follow the plan, put in the preparation and the planning, and leave nothing to chance, this is a mission that can be accomplished in under a week. Pep talk over; let's get on with it.

Operation best seat
PHASE ONE: OBSERVATION

Look at your fellow passengers and notice their dead eyes and blank expressions. Notice the determination to push, shove, and do whatever it takes to get themselves a seat or enough space to open the paper. They're just very bored; the whole thing's been stripped of manners and morals by the corrosive monotony of commuting. Rather than face the crushing tedium as civilized humans, they've switched off and handed the controls to the caveman brain. And for our purposes, this couldn't be better, because bored cavemen are entirely predictable, which makes it easy for the urban bushman to gain the critical edge, and more important, get a seat.

Exercise: Pick three or four travelers at random. Imagine them as hairy savages in bare feet and leopard-print outfits, as they eye each other from beneath prominent brows, and fiddle with their flint axe-heads and iPhones. Retain this image as a constant reminder of whom you're really dealing with here.

PHASE TWO: SURVEILLANCE

Now look at yourself (to help, you may be able to catch a reflection of yourself in the window). Notice how you behave when you're settling in for several stops and when you're about to get off. What are the giveaway signs that reveal your travel plans? You'll start to spot the same things in other passengers. Keeping a backpack on, constantly looking around, shuffling the feet, and zipping up the bag are all signs that you'll be moving soon; taking off a coat or settling into a book without looking up at the stops is a sure sign you're going long haul.

Exercise: Challenge yourself and a travel companion to nominate which passenger from a preselected pool of ten will be getting off next. If you get over 50 percent, you've graduated.

PHASE THREE: PICK YOUR TARGET

Start by studying the seat layout. Identify the best seats and the best spaces—those where you're likely to be most comfortable. You'll begin to realize that there's a hierarchy of seats and standing spaces.

Exercise: Look at the case study that follows, and draw up a plan for your regular bus or train car, with the seats numbered in order of preference. Do the same with the standing spaces. You won't need to think too hard about which seats/spaces are the best; you'll know in your gut. Now that you have a plan on paper, you can devise a strategy to target the best seats.

Straight to the back

When looking for a seat on the bus, head to the back. The back has the highest ratio of seats per square inch, increasing the chance of your getting one when somebody leaves. But do keep in mind that the people at school who used to sit at the back of the bus still tend to sit there these days. And if it's sunny, remember that the back is the hottest part of the bus, since it's nearest the engine.

This makes it the least desirable place to sit, which is good for reducing the competition for seats, but bad if nobody's wearing deodorant.

The hierarchy of seats on the subway

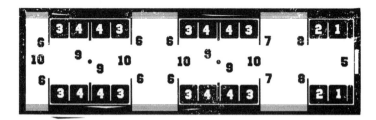

The diagram above shows the seating or standing spots on a subway car, ranked 1-10 in order of tactical superiority. Avoid any unmarked positions. If the bench seats are longer, any middle seats have the same ranking.

SEATED

- **Position 1:** This is the top spot. You have only one neighbor, and the chance of a breeze from the door at the end of the car.
- **Position 2:** Also good, though beware of the person squashed against the glass screen (8). Both 1 and 2 are subjected to less passing traffic than other seats.
- **Position 3:** Less secluded than 2, but still good (only one neighbor).
- **Position 4:** The worst seat (two neighbors, minimal elbow room).

STANDING

- **Position 5:** Comfortable for leaning, with a vantage point over 1 and 2 if they become free, plus fresh air from the door at the end. Nobody can contest this spot, it's yours.
- **Positions 6–8:** Good leaning support and access to a number of seats.
- **Position 9:** No leaning support and only the central pole to hold onto, but a good chance to beat 6 or 7 to a vacated seat.
- **Position 10:** Skillful use of the body to block here can shield seat 3 until it's available to grab.

BATTLE ON THE D

As an occasional visitor to any metropolis, I'm struck by the accomplished and instinctive performance of seasoned subway riders. They sense a change of pace of those ahead of them and know to run for the train. They duck down seemingly blind alleys and corridors only to emerge ahead of the line of the escalator.

It's hardly surprising that seat hierarchy is ingrained in subway culture, as I witnessed on a very crowded car one busy Monday in Manhattan on the D train.

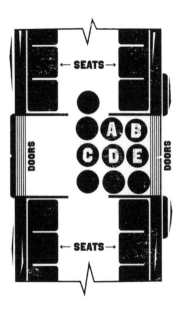

It began at a station when a newcomer stepped into position B (see diagram above) on a crowded car. She had a bad spot near the door and made a bold opening gambit to take position A, one of the best standing positions in the car. She moved forward, trying to shove the woman already at A farther into the car. If she was lucky, her victim wouldn't know the value of her spot.

But this was an experienced commuter, so she countered, pushing the newcomer back against the door. The newcomer shoved back again, but as she did so, a man in the inferior position E made a half-step toward position B. If successful, this would force the newcomer into D, the worst spot of all (nothing to hold onto except other passengers, surrounded on all sides). So she retreated to defend her spot at B.

Suddenly A saw a seat and grabbed it in an instant (this is the great benefit of her position). D had been alert, anticipated the move, and slotted into position behind A in the seamless way only subway commuters can. As for that poor woman at B, I don't think she even noticed.

It was a dance performed in silence, with blank faces and dead eyes. And every day the subway provides drama like this, for anyone tuned in enough to see.

THE GOTHAM SOLSTICE

Every midsummer thousands of people stay up all night to watch dawn break over Stonehenge. It's called the solstice, and people have come to witness the alignment of the rising sun with the ancient stones. Well here's New York City's own equivalent.

It's a product of Manhattan's skewed layout that on most days of the year, you can never look west along a crosstown street to see the sunset. But on two days of the year, the Big Apple and the sun line up just so, and the sun sets exactly across town.

The Gotham Solstice happens on May 28th and July 13th.

MAILING LETTERS THE LAZY WAY

Sending a letter by mail is much harder than it sounds. The first part—writing, filling in a form, enclosing a check—is fine. But it's the next part that's the problem—the actual putting of the thing into the mailbox. Even if you remember to take the envelope with you, it's still in your bag days later, collecting smudges and wrinkles.

The trouble is that mailing letters is a chore. Before e-mail, when everything went by mail, a trip to the post office was part of daily life. There was joy in it because letters were different—white envelopes bulging with personality, addressed in five lines of handwriting, cute and curly or slanted and intriguing. Now it's just tedious.

Here's the solution:

If a letter is dropped in the street any decent person will pick it up, brush it off, and send it on its way via the next mailbox he sees. For some reason letters seem to appeal to our sense of civic duty. And it's this instinctive helpfulness that the British writer of Jeeves and Wooster fame, P. G. Wodehouse,* abused so royally with this system for avoiding trips to the mailbox altogether.

---

* In his memoirs *Bring on the Girls!,* Wodehouse boasted: "It saves me going down four flights of stairs every time I want to mail a letter." That's devilish enough, but we also know that the idea came from a friend, and he was just passing it off as his own. What ho, Wodehouse!

Here it is:

1. Settle into an upstairs study overlooking a street.

2. Write letter.

3. Seal envelope, add address, and stamp.

4. Open window.

5. Throw letter onto street below.

6. Sit back and await reply.

Wodehouse's flash of genius deserves to be revisited, so I've been trying it out. As long as you have the character and the courage to go through with it, it can still work more than fifty years later. But there are a couple of tweaks that will improve your chances.

Although tossing a letter out the window has obvious appeal, the neighbors would get wise to it pretty soon. Here are the golden rules of pavement letter mailing:

- A personal touch is paramount (colorful special edition stamps help). Where possible, avoid brown envelopes and write addresses by hand.

- Drop your letters in a visible spot on the sidewalk. Better still are garden walls, tables outside a café, posh stores, and best of all, a church pew.

- Expect a success rate of 50–60 percent, so only send non-essential letters this way. Where possible, double up each letter and drop twice to improve your chance of success.

How it works

Over the years since Wodehouse, several very helpful psychological studies have added to our knowledge of what works best, together with how and why. In one study, for instance, all the letters were addressed to extremist political organizations. Not surprisingly, they had a lower success rate (30 percent) than letters to individuals (70 percent). Another experiment involved leaving letters on the bus or subway, which was largely successful, but flawed; people would run after the experimenter to give them back the "dropped" letters. The most recent test had a success rate of 55 percent.

Urban bushcraft through the ages: MR. SPOCK

Half human and half Vulcan, the still calm center of the *USS Enterprise,* Spock was a young boy's introduction to the idea that wisdom, control, and serenity can be cool. Though obviously, cool is a word I would never have used in the 1970s when Star Trek was at its peak.

Of all the rainbow coalition of earthlings on board the ship, it was Spock you really wanted to be. Kirk was troubled; he got sweaty, and ripped his shirt. Spock just raised one of those crazy brows. Best of all was his oh-so-special special move. One outstretched hand placed on the collarbone would fell the vilest adversary. The scariest creeps from distant galaxies were all powerless against the Vulcan nerve pinch.

What I love most about Spock is that he shows his superiority over mere humans, not by getting all brainy and complex, but by keeping it simple. He knew his way around all the gadgetry, but when it came down to it, he didn't need any of it. He understood how things worked and he was always ten steps ahead. Kirk was the captain. And when you've got the special moves and know-how, who needs biceps and a bit of gold trim?

3.
THE HUMAN MULTI-TOOL

This special section eases you into the spirit of your new untamed approach to life by acquainting you with the toolbox you get issued just by being human: your own body.

As you discover new ways to measure and record distance and time, these techniques will be your constant companion. As well as helping you cope with some everyday dilemmas, they're great to pull out of your back pocket when you're traveling or when you have bored kids to entertain, or both.

DISTANCE AND TIME— ADVENTURES IN 4-D

To solve everyday problems you need to answer some everyday questions:

- How big is that sofa?
- How far away is that diner?
- How long will it take to get back to the car?
- How long have we lived here?
- How wide is the shelf?
- Will it fit?

Some people would be happy to just guess. Others would wait until they have a tape measure, calendar, or calculator with them. But not you; not now.

With a bit of effort, you can turn your body into a ready reckoner of scale that equips you to tackle any task in four dimensions. Oh yes, four. As well as handling 3-D, you can also measure time; your body comes with a clock, fitted as standard.

THE HUMAN RULER
What you need
Find a piece of string and a ruler or tape measure. As you work through each section, make a note of your personal statistics and keep it somewhere handy, at least until you can remember all the most useful parts.

What it's for

Your aim is to build a system that turns your entire body into a finely calibrated gauge. When you can measure anything using parts of your body, there'll be no more need to remember where you put the tape measure. And that's good news when you need to measure a piece of furniture, carpets, shelving . . . stuff like that.

But this is just the start. You're about to create a four-dimensional toolbox that allows you to calculate much longer distances. You'll be able to tell how far away you are from just about anything, how fast or slow you're going . . . and more.

It's a habit-forming system that gets better and more accurate the more you practice. Early human systems of measurement were all based on anatomical proportions. Now you are reclaiming that concept, linking cold abstract ideas to warm and familiar flesh.

The traditional measure of an inch is the width of a thumb at the bottom of the nail. In French the word for inch and thumb is the same. As it is in Italian, Swedish, Dutch and Sanskrit . . .

How it works

Use your body's natural dimensions as a measuring machine. The width of a thumb, the span of your hand, the length from elbow to tip of index finger (that one is actually the ancient measurement of one cubit). It's best to find the parts of your body that have a memorable whole number measurement.

You may even luck out and find some useful decimal lengths. A good one to start looking for is 4 inches (10 cm). Maybe it's the length of a fingertip to the knuckle, or the width of five fingers, the distance between mole A and mole B. Have fun with a ruler and track it down, preferably somewhere you can access fairly easily. Knuckles, elbows, and knees are useful fixed points.

Now do the same with other distances from 2 to 20 inches (5 to 50 cm). To find a meter, you can use several spans (splayed fingers from thumb to tip of little finger). But the best way is to measure from the tip of the nose to your hand with it stretched out to the side. This is the ancient measure of one yard. It's good for measuring rope and line. If it's not quite long enough, turn your head to one side to gain a few more inches.

You need to be as accurate as possible. To reduce the margin for error, I use a system of averages. For instance, measure four hand spans and divide by four, rather than just measuring it once.

EGYPTIAN MEASUREMENTS

One digit = the width of a finger
Four digits = one palm
Three palms = a small span
Fourteen digits = a large span
Twenty-eight digits = seven palms = one cubit
One cubit = the length from tip of index finger to elbow

Measure your "wingspan"—from fingertip to fingertip with arms outstretched. This is a fathom (6 feet). It's also the same as your height (give or take an inch or two to allow for your freaky variations from normality).

THE REAL DA VINCI CODE

We're built with beautiful symmetry, so we may as well use it. Classical artists made a science of the system of related proportions to which all our bodies conform. Leonardo da Vinci knew all about it (along with most other mysterious secrets of the universe). But right now it's just handy. It helps you to build a consistent set of measurements that's instantly memorable.

> **"Nature has thus arranged the measurements** of a man: four fingers make one palm and four palms make one foot; six palms make one cubit; four cubits make once a man's height; four cubits make a pace, and twenty-four palms make a man's height . . ."
>
> —Leonardo da Vinci (1452–1519)

SIZE OF A COW

In cricket, a bowler instinctively knows if the distance between the wickets looks right. He's used to it. He has that 22-yard pitch marked out in his mind's eye. So cricketers should gauge longer distances on a scale of 22 yards.

Now find your own equivalent. You can already picture the length of your street pretty accurately, the width of your backyard, or the height of your house. So just put them to use. Measure them and store them away as standard measures.

BY THE COLLAR OF YOUR SHIRT

The well-prepared urban bushman can call on most everyday objects to use as measuring tools. If none are available, consider the waistband of your pants (look for the size in the label). I've also used a size-16 shirt collar as a measuring tape.

OTHER APPROXIMATE LENGTHS	
Credit card	2 inches wide (5 cm)
Pen	6 inches (15 cm)
Guitar	3 feet (1 m)
Broom handle	47 inches (120 cm)
Cow	8 feet (2.5 m)
Small car	12 feet (4 m)
Big car	16 feet (5 m)

THE THUMB-OMETER

Measuring long distance by thumb

Having mastered things you can measure by hand, we move on to things that call for a craftier calculation; all those distances you can't measure, such as from here to the car, the local bar, the next busstop, that skyscraper on the horizon, that plane in the sky.

This way of measuring is an ancient system, the original rule of thumb.

> **The thumb-ometer** is the mobile phone of urban bushcraft. Once you've got it, you'll ask yourself what you ever did without it. It has an everyday use for calculating how long it would take to walk from A to B. But, like your new cell phone, you'll just want to keep taking it out of your pocket all day. It's tailor-made for dads to pass on to sons and is also one of the great games for passing the time while waiting at airports.

And it's a valuable part of anyone's urban survival toolbox. It involves doing a small math equation, but the results are well worth any amount of arithmetic.

Stretch out your arm and stick up your thumb. Now close one eye and blot out an object in the distance. Once initiated in the numerology of thumbs, you can work out how far you (and your thumb) are from that object. All you need is one magic number. It holds the answer to the thumb, the universe, and everything. And that number is . . . 30.

Let me explain. With your arm outstretched, the distance between your thumb and your eye is (approximately) 30 thumb widths. That's it. It all flows from there.

AN EXAMPLE

I hold out my arm, with my thumb held on its side horizontally. A distant car appears to be half the height of my thumb's width. Here comes the math. I know cars are generally 5 feet (1.5 m) high, so my thumb appears to be 10 feet (3 m) wide. I now just multiply 10 by that magic number of 30. The result is 300—and so the car is 300 feet (90 m) from my thumb.

The formula is this: distance = apparent size of thumb compared to distant object × 30.

Try it; it works on anything. To test it out, start by standing about 30 feet (9 m) from something that's 1 foot high (0.3 m). Your thumb should completely cover it. At half the distance you need two thumb widths to cover it.

To make this work, all you need is an idea of the standard measurements of the kind of stuff you'll see in your urban habitat. Cars tend to be 5 feet (1.5 m) high, a classic yellow taxi is 15 feet (4.5 m)

5 FEET (1.5 M) X 30 = 300 FEET (91 M)

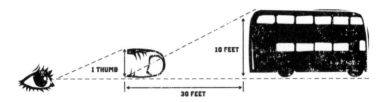

My outstretched thumb appears to blot out a bus. The bus is 10 feet (3 m) high, so I know it's 300 feet (91 m) away.

long, and a single story of a building is 10 to 12 feet (3–3.5 m) high. Oh, and passenger planes tend to be about 150 feet (40 m) from tip to tail.

A few tips:

- Be careful to keep your units of measurement consistent. Whatever you use for the distant object will be the same for the resulting distance.
- For larger things use a fist. The magic number now is 6 (your outstretched arm is 6 fist widths long); for smaller objects use half a thumb, and double the number. Instead of 30, it's 60.

How it works

It's all about triangles and that beautiful gift of proportion. What you're doing is making two similar triangles: a short one from your eye to your thumb, and another from your thumb to the object. You know the angles are all the same and have enough of the measurements to fill in some gaps.

And the number 30 comes into it because although we are all different sizes, we are all in proportion. The relative size of our thumbs (and fists) to the length of our arms tends to be the same—and with your thumb outstretched, it's 30 thumb widths from your eye.

WINKING DISTANCE

There's another way of doing the same thing by winking. All you need to know here is that the distance between your eyes is about a tenth of the length of your arm. So this time what you need to do is put your thumb out, and with one eye shut, line up the nail with one edge of the object. Now swap eyes and your thumb will seem to shift position. Using what you know about the size of a bus, figure out how far your thumb appears to have moved.

If it moved two bus lengths, and a bus is about 30 feet (9 m) long, it moved 60 feet (18 m). Now multiply that by your new magic number: 10. You'll end up with the distance from thumb to bus.

PACE YOURSELF

A formula for measuring distance and speed

This is a system for working out your walking speed, as you go. It comes to us from our old friend Sir Francis Galton. It does what a GPS might do for you, but it's always a joy to show that stuff like this didn't start with the invention of pocket-sized gadgets.

Sir Francis would have used the formula to calculate travel time between river and native village or from camp to the next volcano. Here, it's more likely to serve in finding out whether we'll be at church on time, the cinema before the film starts, or the local bar before closing time.

Say somebody tells you to walk for half a mile, then turn left after the gas station. It only takes a minute or two before you start to have doubts. Have you gone too far? Did you miss it? That's when you're tempted to see if the GPS on your phone can help you figure out how far you've gone. But with this system, you can tell right away. You're walking at 6 mph (10 km), so it will take you 5 minutes.

THE PERSONAL PACE CALCULATOR

STRIDE (INCHES)	TIME (SECONDS)	STRIDE (INCHES)	TIME (SECONDS)	STRIDE (INCHES)	TIME (SECONDS)
21	11.9	31	17.6	41	23.3
22	12.5	32	18.2	42	23.9
23	13.1	33	18.4	43	24.4
24	13.7	34	19.3	44	25.0
25	14.3	35	19.9	45	25.6
26	14.8	36	20.5	46	26.1
27	15.4	37	21.1	47	26.7
28	15.9	38	21.6	48	27.3
29	16.4	39	22.2	49	27.8
30	17.0	40	22.8	50	28.4

All you need to know is the length of your average pace. Then you can keep the GPS on your mobile phone firmly in your pocket. But feel free to use the calculator function to do the little bit of calculation that's needed.

First you need to measure your average stride length (l). The best thing to do is measure out a hundred yards (on a football field or running track). Count how many strides you take (n), then divide 100 by that number (100/n = l) to find the average pace length.

Once you have this length of your average pace, refer to the magic table on page 97, in which Sir Francis worked out, for all stride lengths, how many seconds (s) it would take to make ten paces, traveling at 1 mph (1.6 kmh). This is the golden ticket; one figure that allows you to always work out how fast you're going.

Now, taking this magic number as your personal speed counter, this is what you do:

- Find your pace length on the chart and look for your personal "magic number" of seconds.
- Count the number of paces you take in that number of seconds and divide it by 10.
- If it is 10 paces, you're at 1 mph (1.6 kmh). If 20, then 2 mph (3.2 kmh), if it's 40 or 50 paces . . . then it's 4 or 5 mph (6.4 or 8 kmh).
- More practically, this doesn't often come to round figures. But the formula works to one decimal place, and the math isn't that hard. For instance: My pace length is 34 inches (0.9 cm), so my magic number is 19.3. In that time I count 38 paces. I just divide 38 by 10, to discover I'm walking at a relaxed 3.8 mph (6 kmh).

Urban bushcraft through the ages: Doctor William Bean

When I first heard about William Bean's fingernail clock, I wondered how long he'd been in prison. Staring at four walls for years can lead men to do great things. The storybooks are full of this kind of thing. For a start, there's Casanova's epic escape from prison in Venice using a chisel he'd made from a door bolt. Then there's the birdman of Alcatraz and his 35-year study of diseases of the sparrow. And who could forget the officers of the 51st Highland Division, who used their time in a German POW camp to invent a new country dance.

But then I found out that Doctor William B. Bean had been a free man all his life, a life devoted to the study of fingernail growth. What a guy.

He started his study in 1941. In 1976 he published his magnum opus: *Nail Growth: 35 Years of Investigation.* It's been called the most boring scientific study ever. But in fact it's one of the most thrilling; as you'll soon see.

In 1941 Dr. Bean scratched a line on his thumbnail just above the cuticle and set about timing its progress toward the tip. Then he developed a special system. He'd tattoo his thumbnail each month at the point it emerged and use a specially made gauge to measure its growth. He soon branched out to fingers and toenails, too.

Dr. Bean's revelations are still the last word on the subject. He found the daily rate of growth of the thumbnail is 0.123 mm, with no seasonal variation, and it's staggeringly constant over a lifetime. But this is the bit I love. When he got ill with mumps, his nails slowed down to a halt. Then, when he got better, the growth rate almost doubled, as if to make up for lost time. For all these beautiful revelations, Dr. Bean, we salute you.

If you forget the second number but still have your pace length, then here's another simple formula to give you your speed over the ground:

- You need to know how many steps (n) you take in 5.7 seconds (walk for 17 seconds and divide it by 3).
- Now multiply the number of steps (n) by the length (l) of the pace in inches and divide the answer by 100. The formula is nl/100. For instance, let's say I walk 38 paces in 17 seconds. That's 12.6 in 5.7 seconds.
- My pace length is 40 inches (1 m). 40 (1 m) × 12.6 / 100 = 5. I'm walking at 5 mph (8 kmh).

AT A NAIL'S PACE

There are certain events in life that deserve a monument more personal than an entry in a calendar, and more enduring than a scrawled note on the back of your hand.

With a thumbnail clock you can give singular meaning and worldly gravitas to the passing of time. The ancients had their stone circles and the phases of the moon. Now you can watch the days ebb away at the same speed that continents drift apart.

To make a thumbnail clock

This technique has a whole load of potential applications. The most commonplace way of making it is to score your nail at the cuticle to mark a major event in your life, something like moving or starting a new job. To get kids involved, try making a mark when they start at a new school. No one else in class will have a watch like this. Or they could do it at the same time with all the members of the playground secret agent club. OK guys, synchronize thumbs.

On the first day of your new era, file a furrow along the bottom of the nail, where it emerges from the cuticle. Now you are going to make a device that allows you to take accurate measurements as it progresses up the nail with the reliable constancy of any atomic clock.

You need a matchbox, some graph paper or any calibrated scale, and some glue.

A thumbnail clock

Here's how:

1. Remove the matchbox "tray" and cut off one end.

2. Now place the digit to be monitored into the open end, all the way so that the tip rests against the other end. For extra precision, draw a line around it so that you can put it back in the exact same position each time.

3. Cut away enough of the matchbox's sliding "lid" to reveal the whole nail length, but leaving the sides of the nail hidden.

4. Stick your measuring gauge or graph paper to the remaining sides. These are now the "gauge" and should rest nicely along the length of the nail.

The clock is now ready. Using the Bean constant of 0.123 mm per day, you can mark 10-day periods along the gauge. Or each time you take a measurement, use the constant to calculate the elapsed number of days.

THE THUMBNAIL COUNTDOWN

Here's a thumbnail timer that doesn't depend on building the clock. This technique is for when you want a constant reminder of approaching events. If you're lucky enough to have a thumbnail that's around 0.5 inches (1.2 cm) long, you will be able to follow a mark as it travels the whole length of your nail, and to know when 100 days has passed. But for most of us, it's safer to mark 100-day periods in reverse, from the top of the nail down.

Take care to measure from where the "white" of the nail tip starts, rather than from the tip itself. This allows you to continue on cutting your nails without upsetting the calibration.

Just make a mark on your nail at 0.5 inches (1.2 cm) down, 100 days before the big day, and watch your deadline approaching.

This is an especially good way of reminding yourself about particularly dreadful things. I use it to watch the approach of the April 15th tax deadline. The impending dark clouds are brightened by the joy of watching the process work. It softens the blow.

CHILDREN'S COUNTDOWN TIMER

If you can get children involved, this is a great way to deal with the endless questioning about how long there is until a birthday or Christmas.

In my experience, the questions begin to intensify with about a month to go. So to nip them in the bud, just measure your child's nail, and using the 0.1 mm-a-day rule, make a mark at a spot 5 mm or (50 days) from the end. Done. The answer to their question is on hand, literally, whenever they want to check.

NAIL GROWTH IN ORDER OF SPEED (FASTEST FIRST)

Thumb
Finger
Big toe
Other toes

4.
CITY
ADVENTURES

Every tribe mourns its past, and we city dwellers are no different. We liked things the way they were; we always have. But there's a difference between a fondness for the familiar and plain pig-headed resistance to change; that's a dead end you don't want to go down. Adapting to new habitats and new surroundings is what we do best, and besides, it's what urban bushcraft is all about.

One pet peeve of the anti-progress league is the modern main street with its homogeneous storefronts and multiple chain stores. They're all the same, they say. And indeed they are—very good observation. But instead of moaning and signing petitions, the urban bushman sees all this as a big fat opportunity. Instead of getting worn down by the lines and the lack of a place to pee, he grasps this chance to do what he does best: to rise above the herd and strike out on his own.

Amid the bored shoppers along the main street and the mind-altering marketing messages of the mall, he can craft a city adventure. By retuning the tribal antenna, he blocks out the big branded bribes and picks up the timeless wisdom beneath. This, after all, is his domain; it's what thousands of years of progress have been leading to, and now is the time to make the most of it. Let's go to town.

HOW TO PREDICT THE WEATHER WITH A CUP OF COFFEE

This is an ageless technique that's especially satisfying when you pull it off among the laptops and body piercings of a twenty-first century coffee shop.

A mall is a good place to practice some earth science, and a coffee break is a good time to check the likelihood of rain. If you've just ducked in for shelter, then this should help you decide whether to make a beeline for the bus before it gets worse, or relax and order another while the skies clear. Of course, you could just listen to an up-to-date weather report, but then you could just drink instant coffee, and you don't. This is lifestyle weather forecasting. Back in the America of the Waltons, this way of predicting the weather was as familiar as dungarees and moonshine.

Here's how to:

1. Take a cup of black coffee (made from beans).

2. Drop a lump of sugar to the bottom of the cup.

3. Don't stir or disturb the coffee.

4. Watch the bubbles rise to the surface.

5. Notice where bubbles gather.

How to read your coffee barometer:

- Bubbles in the middle: FINE WEATHER

- Bubbles around the rim: RAIN OR SNOW

- Bubbles all over the place: CHANGEABLE

FINE WEATHER

RAIN OR SNOW

CHANGEABLE

How it works

The tiny air bubbles in the sugar lump are released as the sugar dissolves. The high pressure that keeps the skies clear and the weather fair pushes down on the center of the coffee, making the surface curve down at the middle, so the bubbles hit the middle first and gather there.

Low pressure, indicating clouds and rain, works like a vacuum, pulling up the center of the drink, so the bubbles gather at the edges.

The behavior of the bubbles in the fluid is particular to coffee and is caused by the surface tension and slight oiliness from the beans.

TIPS

- Don't try this in frappé-style iced drinks. The heat of the coffee improves the performance—something to do with surface tension.
- Milk is the enemy of the reliable barometer. We're not looking for froth here but for those tiny golden bubbles you get in a rich black coffee. The best weather forecasters drink either Americano or a simple espresso.

FOR MINI METEOROLOGISTS

Set up restless children with their own weather station in an espresso cup. Get them to make observations as they drop in a lump of sugar every five minutes, to be repeated three times. It should keep them busy while you catch up on the sports section of the paper.

THE SPECIAL FORCES APPROACH TO CUSTOMER COMPLAINTS

Elite training in the secret techniques for cracking the call center

Calling customer service is one of the toughest tests of nerve that modern life has to offer. So naturally it's an irresistible opportunity for the urban bushman to practice his art. First, let's study what's going on.

On the other end of the phone, there's a mindless automaton reading from a script. Then, if you get past him, you face the well-drilled specialist with pat responses that deflect all your questions until you lose the will to live. This is a one-on-one confrontation, a mental chess game where you have to hold firm while your opponent does all he can to grind you down.

What's needed here is a system to give you the strength to endure and help you to keep your goal in sight. That's what I was looking for when the answer hit me. It was shining straight at me like a spotlight in a bare cell: the SAS anti-interrogation drill.

"Anti-interrogation" is an SAS specialty. On top-secret missions behind enemy lines, there's always a chance of capture, so it's essential they don't crack under questioning. In training, SAS soldiers are drilled in the seven essentials of anti-interrogation. And with a bit of minor adaptation, this same code of conduct can become a guide to customer complaints that'll turn you into a call-center maestro. The symmetry between the two scenarios is

> **The Special Forces system** can be applied to any customer-services confrontation: insurance companies, mortgage lenders, cell phone operators, or a customer-complaints desk.
>
> Life as a consumer is generally fairly straightforward. But then something goes wrong, and it all changes; you've been overcharged, blatantly ripped off or misled, and you need to call and complain. And suddenly life turns into a scene in an airport thriller.
>
> The clock ticks. Beads of sweat jostle for position on your forehead. You stare at the phone, and it stares right back. All you can think about is making the call. You pick it up and start to dial. You've done this ten times already, only this time you won't hang up; you'll see it through to the end.
>
> Click. The phone answers and you wait for the dreaded voice. You flinch; here it comes: "For questions about your bill..." You press 2 just to make it stop. Another beep... "All of our representatives are busy. Please wait while we connect your call..." Your strength is fading.
>
> You want to give up, but you have to go on. Then it happens... it's the hold music. No, please... anything but that!

uncanny. Whether you're an SAS soldier facing a grueling interrogation or the urban bushman calling a complaints line, this is the best briefing you'll get.

RULE 1

SAS: Accept the situation you're in; you're likely to suffer, and it will be a long process.

Urban bushman: Don't let the cheesy music, the jargon, and the recorded messages get to you; resolve to see your money-back mission through to the end.

RULE 2

SAS: Keep your mental integrity—it's the one thing you can control.

Urban bushman: Don't ever say, "Actually it's fine, I'm probably just overreacting."

RULE 3

SAS: Be "the gray man." Never get aggressive or stand out.

Urban bushman: Don't be rude or curt, keep the moral high ground.

RULE 4

SAS: Beware of a switch to softer tactics and claims that they're just trying to help you. This is designed to make you talk.

Urban bushman: If they start calling you "sir" and offering apologies from the manager, don't buckle; stick to your demands.

RULE 5

SAS: Overplay any injuries they cause you, even cry.

Urban bushman: Maintain your outrage at every stage of the process. Make sure they know how inconvenient all this is. Complain about the frustration of waiting on hold.

RULE 6

SAS: Use eye-to-eye contact. Make them identify with you.

Urban bushman: Get the name of the rep you're dealing with, and use it.

Ask them directly for help; a personal element can work where all else fails.

RULE 7

SAS: "What if . . ." Plan ahead and be ready to react if things change.

Urban bushman: Prepare your responses for any eventuality. Be ready for them to make a token offer, reject your complaint, or refer you to the manager . . . don't let them surprise you into agreeing to anything.

THE MALL OF THE WILD

The mall is a machine for turning people into shoppers. First it unsettles us with its anodyne atmosphere, then it lures us in with a powerful piece of tribal persuasion. Once he's understood the forces at work, the urban bushman can have fun eluding its grasp.

To do that, though, we need to understand how the two-part process works.

PART ONE: THE NOMAD IN THE MALL

The old-fashioned street with lampposts and a gutter is a place where people feel at home. It's somewhere to flirt and burp and do as you please. But how different things are when we hit the mall. On the face of it, this place is designed for our comfort and delight, with its fountains, piazzas, and coffee-bar atriums. But nobody ever feels at home here, do they? Not really. I always think shoppers in malls have the look of an uninvited horde at a glitzy wedding. You can see it in their eyes; they're trying to blend in but failing.

Think about it like this: If you had a ball on the street, you'd give it a few bounces. If there weren't any cars coming, you might even play a game of catch. On the street you can tie up your dog, chain up your bike, and act as you please. But not in the mall, not ever.

It all comes down to the big central purpose; this place is for shopping. Like an airport, it's where people are processed; they become a throughput, never a population. In the mall we're nomads, we can't settle, and that's a pretty soulless experience for a territorial animal like man.* At least in an airport there's that little room where you can go and pray (far better value than the first-class lounge, by the way). In the mall there's nothing to do but to shop, and so you're ready for part two.

PART TWO: THE TRIBAL TRAP

Back when our tribal village was just a hundred strong, it was important to show we knew the rules and that we'd fit in just fine. We needed everyone to know that we were on the level, and over the centuries it became a habit. Nowadays, most of the people that surround us are completely irrelevant to our lives, but we still like them to think we're part of the gang. It's just another survival strategy that's outlived its purpose. And it comes to the fore in the mall.

---

* Next time you go to a mall, try this. Claim a bit of territory by setting up camp just like at the airport when you're waiting for a delayed departure. Take turns to make shopping forays and come back to base. Now doesn't that feel better? Told you so.

Softened up and unsettled, we're at our most shallow and vulnerable. Then we're offered membership to a club, a tribal identity, and a way to fit in with the crowd, so we grab it.

Every retailer on the main street works hard at telling us that buying makes us belong. It's why shops create a mood, a lifestyle to aspire to. Membership is formalized with a flurry of rituals, little branded blessings if you like, all giving the process an inflated over-importance. Your purchase is adoringly wrapped, then there's the congratulatory chit-chat, and finally comes the oversized shopping bag with its handles of silken cord. A little sticky fastener at the top seals the deal and you're ready to go, sent out like a missionary to spread the good word.

The best and simplest demonstration of all this is the tribalism at work in the market for fast food and coffee to go, where the badge of belonging is a bright yellow burger box or a branded paper cup. Here's how it works.

Professor Latte

Bryant Simon from Philadelphia's Temple University has studied why people buy coffee at Starbucks prices when they really don't need to. He breaks the reasons into three categories: the "functional" (serving a coffee addiction); the "emotional" (giving ourselves a treat); and, for him the most powerful, the "expressive" (showing the world we can afford luxury). Before you know it, Starbucks is issuing branded paper cups to six million people a day, all desperate to tell the world they belong.

Starbuckers

Starbuckers (as I call them) feel comfortable in their club because of a strictly policed demographic profile; this is a sanctuary for the comfortably off in their late teens to mid-40s, and nobody else dares enter. The oldies are turned off by the decor, the music, and the pierced eyebrows of the servers, while the high price of a coffee keeps away the delinquents and the buy-rite brigade in cheap clothing.

We are all suckers for some tribal seduction and an open invitation to belong. But we aren't complete morons. A logo and a storefront alone aren't enough to have us clamoring to enlist. We want to be wooed with a bit of hoodoo, some ritual, and some exciting new language. So that's just what the main street's biggest brands give us. Starbucks or McDonald's—just walk in and you're under the spell of the tribal language, the customs, the music, and the brand. Skinny lattes, oddly shaped trays, stubby little pens, happy meals—it's a hypnotic ritual conducted by witch doctors in green aprons or red caps, and the Stone Age brain instantly wants to be in on it. Look over there! Who's that loser who doesn't know where the coffee stirrers are?

The art of not belonging

This is a simple way of restating your identity in the mall. I use it as a kind of reboot whenever the urge to buy into the brands gets too strong. And it's a good demonstration of how strong the tribal persuasion can be.

The moment of ordering is the key to tribal belonging. By using that special language, you're swearing allegiance and joining the club. It's a little piece of theater that bonds you to the brand.

Now think how it would feel to go into McDonald's and calmly order a pizza with extra mushrooms. Or ask a pierced barista in Starbucks for a chicken chow mein? If you don't think you could do it, all the more reason to try. If nothing else, it will give you a ten-second rush of adrenaline, like a mini–bungee jump.

Here's what you do:

- First select your target—the kind of place that puts employees in uniforms and uses the TM logo on words they've made up on the menu. Starbucks works well on all counts.
- Once you've picked your spot, don't hesitate. Just walk in and wait to be served.
- When you get to the front of the line, look the assistant in the eyes and calmly and politely ask for a cheeseburger with fries.
- They may pretend they didn't hear or ask you to repeat it, so ask again. Say it as if it's the most natural thing in the world: cheeseburger with fries, please.
- When they tell you they don't have any, just thank them and leave.

As you head for the door, feel the excitement build. You did it. You broke the power of the tribe. The best part is nobody's about to cast you into the wilderness. That's because it wasn't really a tribal ceremony at all, just a coffee chain wanting to charge over $4 for a cup of foamy milk.

Obviously if you do this too much, you'll start to be branded as a nut, which wouldn't do anyone any good.

Sock solutions

You're walking home from the supermarket and the handles of your bags have turned to cheese wire. They've cut furrows across your fingers that make you want to cry, with half a mile to go and no bus in sight. Don't worry, comfy grip relief can be yours. Just take off a sock and wind it around the handle; it works great.

Those junk "flyers" that fall out of newspapers are also useful for this (and for nothing else).

THE WHITE COFFEE CHALLENGE

Here's another version of the same thing; it's simpler but still fun. Go into any big coffee chain with a friend and order a drink without using any words from their special lexicon. They speak English, don't they? Try asking for a "white coffee" for instance. If you manage to get your drink without using any of the forbidden words during the entire exchange with staff, your friend pays.

Mission milk

The milk at a supermarket is always at the back, in the far corner. The idea is that you'll be distracted on the way and find yourself with a shopping cart full of premium-priced goodies. It's passive manipulation of your mind and your wallet. Your mission, should you choose to accept it, is to buy a single carton of milk, and nothing else. If you succeed, congratulate yourself on your resolve. This country needs people like you.

The $5 card limit

When you have no ready cash and an urgent need for a coffee, be prepared for the cashier's mantra: "Sorry, there's a $5 limit on credit cards."

Don't even stop to think; it's time to make a friend. Simply turn to one of those caffeine-starved strangers walking in, wanting to buy coffee. Remember to be bright but matter of fact as you say, "Hi, can I buy you a coffee?" He'll laugh and look confused.

This is where you have to be reassuring; act like you do this every day. Explain that you need to pay by credit card but there's a $5 limit (you can show your exasperation here a bit, because you can bet he's been in the same boat) and finish it off with something pleasant like, "So if you've got the cash for yours, I'll get the coffees." He'll laugh again and hand over the money, either impressed by your ingenuity or too caffeine deprived to argue.

If it doesn't all come to a fiver, and it probably does, buy a muffin. You decide who gets the bonus card with its double stamp. And remember, the more convincing and calm you are, the more likely it is that the chosen stranger will stick to the script.

TOILET WISDOM

Sooner or later you're going to have to find a bathroom. We all know about the bathrooms in department stores, public libraries, and bookstores. You probably have your own network of preferred sites, but here are a couple of tips.

THE UPGRADE

Think about it: Every hotel has bathrooms somewhere near reception, and the doorman has no idea who's staying at the hotel. (Yes, I said doorman. We're not talking about the local Holiday Inn here.) Pick a big hotel, as swanky as you like. If it's a tourist hotel, big shopping bags and cameras help you blend in. If it's a businessman's favorite, then make an effort to blend in. This all suits the urban bushman because it's a bit like getting an upgrade on a plane; play the part, pull it off with panache, and your reward is a touch of first-class comfort.

I find this especially useful at train stations, where the big Sheraton or Hilton always has an international cast of hundreds milling around looking for their colleagues. Instead of looking for Wayne from marketing, you're desperately seeking something else, but who'd really know.

STALL CHOICE

Psychologists tend to agree that in public bathrooms there is a tendency to go to the stall farthest from the door first. As a result, the nearest stall is usually the cleanest and least used. If this were a dog race, your money should be on trap one.

THE ATM LINE (AND HOW TO CUT IT)

The line for the ATM is a special case because of three little quirks all of its own. You need to know this, whether you're planning to cut or simply defending your rightful place.

A. THE MULTIPLE LINE DECEPTION

With two or more ATMs, the norm is to form a single line, so that the person at the front goes to the first machine that's free. But it's only a convention, not a rule, and as a result this line is at risk from the suggestion that each ATM should have a line of its own.

Tactics

Let's start with the easiest target of all—a single person waiting in a line of one when there's more than one ATM. Just draw an imaginary line between the ATMs across the floor and see which side of it the person is standing on (person waiting). Very calmly take your position alongside them, on the other side of this line (you).

As far as this person knows, you simply assumed that there are two lines, one for each ATM. Since there's not a lot at stake, he's unlikely to argue. If challenged, this is easy to pass off as a simple mistake. Where more ATMs are available, this maneuver is even easier.

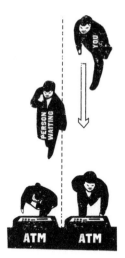

Bad positioning—unclear.

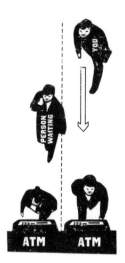

Defense—to prevent any ambivalence, adopt a wide stance firmly in the middle of the machine.

B. THE COURTESY GAP

Convention dictates that the first in line leaves a "courtesy gap" behind the person at the ATM so that he doesn't feel threatened or overlooked. But this can be misinterpreted by people joining the line. On crowded sidewalks, it's normal to allow passing pedestrians through this gap, adding to the uncertainty.

Tactics

If the courtesy gap is too large, stand between this person and the ATM, as if you hadn't seen them. Avoid eye contact. There's a good chance they'll avoid any confrontation and simply move in behind you. As above, this is easily passed off as a simple mistake.

Defense

Keep the courtesy gap to less than 5 feet (1.5 m). The person waiting was there first, but you are able to move in, easily owing to multiple line deception and the courtesy gap being too large.

C. FRIENDS IN THE SAME LINE

When people stand in a line with others who may or may not be taking out money, it's hard to judge who's in the line and who isn't.

Opportunity: This always causes confusion so there's a chance to line up in front of one or both, on the supposed assumption that they're just waiting for a friend.

DEFENSIVE POSTURES

This simple code deters anyone with an eye on your place in the line.

- **Sideways stance:** This allows you to hold a place and face down any challenger.
- **Eye contact:** A shrewd challenger avoids eye contact; don't let him escape it.
- **Micro movements:** The slightest shuffle can signal your intentions and make clear how the line is working—normally enough to warn off any potential challenger.

THE SECRET LIFE OF A LINE

Lining up is something humans do all over the world, without a second thought. If you weren't particularly switched on, you could see it as a great civilizing force, a system of cooperation held together by a shared sense of natural justice. But the urban bushman knows better than that and doesn't believe it for a second. Once you know the truth about this strange convention, then exploring it further is impossible to resist—especially when it can be turned to your advantage.

Just as there are little tricks you can train animals to do to demonstrate a simple piece of behavior, so there are with humans. Put a wood louse in the light, and he'll run toward darkness. Draw a chalk line across an ant's trail, and he won't cross it. Start a line in front of human beings and some of them will join it. Try it with a few friends. Just form a line in front of a store and see how long it takes before people start to join the end.

THE LAW OF WAITING IN LINE

I didn't use to cut. But then I had a revelation, standing in the line at a crowded airport check-in. There were tour groups and luggage carts everywhere, but at least it was a line, so there was some sense of order. Then suddenly everything changed, as a sea of people rushed to join a newly opened check-in lane. A family of seven that was way behind me in the original line was now way up there in front. In fact the whole line seemed to be composed of people who were once back where I was. Now they were up there, where I wasn't. And nobody complained. First come, first served? Forget it. This was a perfect demonstration of the secret code of lines.

Rule 1: There are no rules

Lines pretend to be all about fair play, upholding the rule of first come, first served. But that's not how it is. That's just how we like things to look until there's a chance to get to the front. When it breaks down, the line's real nature is revealed; it's every man for himself. In the airport nobody expects the line to split fairly and move across to the newly opened lane in nice orderly sections. Anyone who can get to the front is applauded.

This is one of many wrinkles in the system that has developed over the millennia since Noah made his animals go two by two. We think of line cutters as the enemy, the rotten apples in the barrel, but if you pick your moment and take your chance, line cutting can be seen as a noble art.

THE SEVEN SECRETS OF CUTTING

Psychologists love lines and love testing our behavior when we're in them, and their research provides a pretty good guide to cutting. Nearly all the studies show that people who cut aren't challenged as often as you might think. And by digging a bit deeper, you start to discover what tactics increase the chances of getting away with cutting. It's a valuable resource that is best remembered as the seven secrets.

1. Single file

Single-file lines, where people stand one behind another, are the easiest to cut. In these lines, social order is weaker because there's no eye contact. Just slide in and stand facing forward.

In a long line, then, look for any part of it where people are standing in single file.

2. Excuse me

Of all the experiments relating to lines, the one in the 1980s by American psychologist Stanley Milgram recorded the lowest rate of complaints about blatant cutting—constantly below 50 percent and sometimes as low as 10 percent. Ask yourself: If you knew there was only a 10 percent chance of someone saying something, would you go for it? Me, too. So here's the secret. As they cut, all of Milgram's line cutters just said, "Excuse me, I'd like to get in here," and stood in line, facing forward.

3. Back is best

The best hunting ground is toward the back. Though there's less to gain, success is far more likely. At the front, people become a tight-knit clique, likely to notice an impostor. But at the back, it's all far less organized, and far less suspicious (people expect line cutters to target the front).

For all they know, someone who merges with confidence could be returning to his rightful spot. Join the line confidently a third of the way from the back, and you'll soon be accepted as one of them.

4. Be first

Don't merge in where others have done so already, since there's a much higher chance of people objecting. A one-time exception is sometimes accepted, but multiples rarely are. It's all because a line accepts a certain amount of law breaking, on the basis that once the lawbreaker is in the line, the correct order is restored, and the line becomes stronger. But if a lot of people were to try it, the whole line could break down, so people are forced to say something.

5. Bide your time

A line assumes that the longer somebody's been waiting, the more he deserves a reward. But time keeping can be a bit vague, and it doesn't take too long before someone who has just shown up in a line can start to accumulate points and be seen as a deserving case. If you cut, it sometimes takes only ten or fifteen minutes of waiting before you, too, are seen as a valid member of the line, sharing the pain of waiting with those who might have been there for hours.

6. The brace

Waiting in line is painful because we see it as time down the toilet, lost and gone forever. But the bushman in the line uses every second and all his senses to be alert to whatever opportunities present themselves. If nothing else, it passes the time. And he knows that every line has its moment, just like the airport line, when you can cut without being seen as a cheat.

The best chance presents itself at what I call the "brace"—that moment when the line tenses as it starts to move—perhaps the checkout has just been manned or the barriers have been opened. Everyone squeezes closer and cranes to see what's happening. This is the moment to pounce. Everyone's far too busy guarding their space to notice, and the brace has broken any social bonds forged between neighbors in the line.

7. Know your line

The line you can never jump is the "who's next?" line. Here, there's no line, just a tacit agreement based on our incredible ability to remember the order of people who came after us. I've encountered this most recently waiting at a parking garage, but it's common in all kinds of waiting rooms, stores, and offices. Without a word, everyone understands their role: to remember who has come after them. By a process of deduction, when only these stragglers are left, you know you're next. It's genius. And it can't be cracked.

The system at the bar is a version of this, when everyone knows who's next. But there's an added element of competition to see who can trick the bartender into serving them before their turn. It's cutting by mutual consent, where skill at getting served is more valued than time spent waiting.

DOS AND DON'TS AT THE BAR

The urban bushman can override years of experience in hanging out at the bar with this back-of-a-beer-mat guide:

- Put a hand on the bar, even if it has to snake through a crowd to get there.
- Eye contact with bar staff is crucial; they'll remember you if you smile.
- Point to someone at the bar to signal they're next. You'll be served after them.
- No coin tapping or money waving—that's just annoying.
- No shouting out or complaining. Bar staff are well practiced at ignoring people like you.

THE OPTIMISTIC LINE

My favorite psychological test for showing the complexity of line behavior is the one performed on people waiting for a limited number of tickets, where everyone in line is asked what chance they think they have of getting a ticket. For instance, in one line for 140 tickets, questioners asked every 10th person in line how many people they thought were ahead of them. The first few were fairly accurate. Then, after 30 people or so, people started to over-estimate the number of those in front of them. That went on until about 130, just where the ticket allocation would start to run out. Here people suddenly became more optimistic and started to underestimate the numbers ahead of them.

The same test has been done several times with the same result; people near the back consistently overestimate their chances, and inflated optimism starts to be shown at around the exact point where the cutoff will fall. One theory says that these people would have to be among life's optimists to have joined the line so far back in the first place.

LINE UP THE DISNEY WAY

Disney theme park teams are experts at making people happy to line up for the big rides. They put up signs giving wait times that are purposely overestimated by 10 minutes or so. That way, when a 40-minute wait ends, people feel pleased they didn't have the anticipated 50-minute wait. Try it on the family next time they ask how long it'll be till you get there.

ATM TRACKING

If you ever stop to think about it (and believe me, I do), it's hard to fathom the logic of where ATMs are located. There just don't seem to be any hard-and-fast rules. The answer is to stop thinking and trust your urban instinct. Experience teaches you where to expect a cash machine. You can't explain what you're looking for, but you recognize the right conditions when you see them. Your brain has processed the information and drawn up a profile; it just doesn't bother you with the details. The best you can come up with are vague statements like, "This looks like the right kind of street." But don't be discouraged: Trust your brain because it's right.

As far as I can see, the profile assimilated by your unconscious over years of looking for an ATM is exactly the same as the one the banks use. You know what looks like the right kind of street, but you just haven't felt the need to rationalize it. The banks do, of course, and the result is the same.

It all comes down to safety. Not the safety of customers, but the safety of the men who put the money in. You see, banks don't want the ATM to be raided, or the men who fill it to be held up at gunpoint. So they stick to areas that fit the profile. And tell me these features aren't the same as those in your mind, if you really can:

Criteria for an ATM location:

- low-crime area
- no areas of concealment where assailants might hide
- well lit
- monitored by CCTV
- good access for vehicles

If an area fits those criteria, it's an ATM zone, and where you find one machine, there are probably others. By the way, I'm not talking about the cash machines that you find in corner stores that look more like a novelty money box. The criteria for those are the opposite of the above.

THE SIDEWALK TANGO

Two people approach each other on the sidewalk and try to get out of each other's way, but instead they enter into a strange dance, each one mirroring the other, shuffling left and right, making it impossible to pass. This familiar and uncomfortable phenomenon is the face-off that was joyfully designated "a droitwich" by authors Douglas Adams and John Lloyd. It's the pedestrian equivalent of a stammer. A few people have tried to find a way to break the cycle but, until now, I haven't read of one who has gotten it right.

First of all, forget any suggestion that on the sidewalk we obey a highway code, driving on the left or right depending on the law of the land. If that were true, the droitwich would never happen. The pedestrian in the right would simply stick to his guns, just as in most traffic collisions. The problem comes when two men make their move at the same moment. Both would rather avoid a face-off so both make the concession and step inside, and the droitwich is complete.

On the sidewalk, we plan passing moves way ahead. Decisions are based on an advanced negotiation as each party makes tiny shows of intention, beamed along the pavement. We're so used to all this that we barely think about it. This is why a droitwich commonly occurs when you turn a corner—there's been no chance for the negotiation to take place.

What's really happening is a bit like being sucked into a vortex, as conflicting forces collide: manners and convention, impatience and embarrassment, learned behavior and instinct. And rather than solve it, I prefer to celebrate this glorious revelation of the wonderful complexity at work in everyday actions.

NUT JITSU

People who walk around the city at night shouting and threatening to punch people's lights out may tell you they're afraid of nothing. But it's not true. We are all afraid of loonies. I really don't mean mental illness in any clinical sense here; I mean the concept that we had in the playground of a real nut. Someone who starts spouting gibberish just makes us feel uneasy. A very high proportion of us would simply rather not be around such a person.

This rather ungenerous trait is worth remembering if you're ever unfortunate enough to be physically threatened by a an intimidating stranger. Don't answer any of the inevitable questions ("You looking at me?" etc.). He knows what you're going to say, because he's heard all the rational answers before. Say something he's never heard before. Engage him, clearly and brightly, with irrelevant nonsense dug up from your childhood, or the last story you read the kids at bedtime. Just be normal, but talk nonsense. It should seem as if there's a burning issue that perhaps he can help you with: the mystery of the purple clouds, whether the taxis are giant beetles, anything like that. It should confuse things long enough for him to forget exactly why he wanted to punch you in the first place. And you'll probably settle for that.

5.
WHEN DISASTER STRIKES

The urban bushman doesn't deal with the kind of emergency that you may see described elsewhere; you know the kind of thing, the collapse of civilization, global apocalypse, and all that stuff.* It's just not his main concern. What bothers him much more are the disasters he confronts from day to day: the broken coffee machine, no lighters for the barbecue, having forgotten the combination to that cheap lock, and having to carry a load of

---

* In the unlikely event that you find yourself in a post-apocalyptic survival scenario, here's what you do: Locate a survivor wearing belted shorts and a smug grin (he'll probably be weaving fish traps or building a canoe from the bark of a tree). Now ask for a light. He'll be so keen to demonstrate his ability to spark up an ember that you'll have just enough time to swipe his gear. No need to feel guilty; after all, he was the one who wanted to live by his wits.

laundry to the laundromat when the bag isn't big enough. What he wants are real solutions for real crises.

The following starter kit will help you reach a state of total readiness from which you can build up your own repertoire of techniques and prepare for all eventualities (barring global disaster, of course).

THE URBAN FIRE STARTING KIT

Forget lighters and a big box of matches; all you need for an effortless fire every time (and always in a controlled nonflammable environment) is a Brillo pad (or some steel wool) and a battery. The 9-volt battery is the kind that goes into radios, and it's best for the job simply because the terminals are both on the same end. Toilet paper is the standard item to use as tinder, but anything that burns quickly and easily will do. Hold the Brillo pad loosely at one end and dab the other end onto the terminals. It will start to glow and fizz immediately. Just touch a few sheets of toilet paper onto it and blow to encourage the flames.

Despite the similarity in appearance, this doesn't work with shredded wheat.

How it works

As soon as the wire touches the terminals, it makes a circuit. Electricity flows through the tiny strands of steel wool, making them so hot that they glow red and start to burn. It's the same principle as Edison's ingenious light bulb, as demonstrated by him in 1879.

He used a tungsten filament and put it in a vacuum so it couldn't burn, only glow.

This does drain power from the battery. A 9-volt battery can light a few fires, but on a week-long camping trip be prepared to go through a few of them.

NO STEEL WOOL? NO PROBLEM, USE A CAR BATTERY . . .

Holding them safely, attach some jump leads to the battery in the normal way and prepare a little ball of tinder. Put the tinder on the ground and quickly touch the terminals together with the tinder. The sparks will easily be enough to get a glowing ember or two, and with a few little puffs, a flame. Cotton wool, upholstery straw, the lint from inside a parka, belly button lint—any of these will do.

LIFE WITHOUT MATCHES

The friction match was invented in 1827. But for tens of thousands of years up to that point, lighting a fire was a skill touched by magic and mystery. Flints and fire starters were cherished possessions. And most appealing of all, lighting fires was something men could be good at. So it's hardly surprising that, despite its new-found convenience, the fire-lighting ritual lost none of its man appeal, whether it was in the Western legend of cowboys striking matches on their stubble or using the rugged gas-guzzling Zippo lighter. Fire is man's greatest technological triumph, and we're always going to have a weakness for staring into the flames.

It's summed up pretty well by Ellsworth Jaeger, an authority on Native American bushcraft, in his 1945 book, *Wildwood Wisdom:* ". . . whether we realize it or not all our ancestral memories come surging to the surface from the depths of our beings when we sit around the campfire. We, too, are stirred by its magic, even as were our shadowy ancestors long ago." Absolutely, Ellsworth . . . now pass me a Brillo pad.

STARTING A FIRE WITH A COKE CAN AND A CHOCOLATE BAR

This little secret is popular with kids, but it's still a bona fide grown-up technique. You could wait a long time for a genuine need to light a fire using the contents of a lunch box, so grab the chance next time you've got an urge to experiment. The classic way into this is to present someone with the can and chocolate and challenge him to light a fire.

What you need:

- a soda can
- chocolate bar
- tinder (as mentioned earlier, the lint from inside a parka works well)
- sunshine

How it works

The sunshine gives it away. It's a version of the old Boy Scout trick where you use a magnifying glass to burn ants, but just a lot better. The secret ingredients are the can's concave bottom and the magical polishing properties of chocolate. Put them both together, and you'll have a mirror that can focus the sun's rays into an intense spot of light able to get your tinder smoking in seconds.

Use little lumps of chocolate just like shoe polish on the bottom of the can, rubbing hard with the wrapper until it starts to shine. Work at it until it's so shiny you get crazy "hall of mirrors" reflections in the can. It will take half an hour or so, but you'll get there—it's all to do with the slightly abrasive properties of chocolate. Any type of chocolate will do, the purer the better.

DO NOT eat the chocolate after use! It picks up aluminum from the can, which is toxic.

Now that the lens is ready, you need to find the focal point. One good way is to use a scrap of newspaper that's white on one side and heavily printed on the other. Point the can at the sun and hold the paper so that the white side is toward the can. On the black side you should see a spot of light. Move the paper closer and farther away from the can to find the point where the spot is smallest. That's the focal point, as you'll see when the paper starts to smolder.

Bunch up the chocolate wrapper and put it in the middle of a nest of tinder: twigs, leaves, or anything that will burn. Focus the beam on your tinder, and as soon as it starts to smoke, encourage it to flame by gently blowing on it.

If you're doing everything right, it should take five seconds or so until the wrapper is setting fire to your nest of tinder.

If the polishing takes too long with chocolate, and you think you can live with yourself afterward, there are other quicker options. But beware, there's a law of diminishing returns: As the polishing agent becomes more effective, the primal job satisfaction is diminished. It becomes less bushcraft, more DIY.

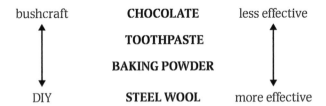

bushcraft   **CHOCOLATE**   less effective

TOOTHPASTE

BAKING POWDER

DIY   **STEEL WOOL**   more effective

HOW TO TURN YOUR PANTS INTO A BACKPACK

You run into a supermarket to get a quart of milk, then you pick up a few other things until you've got both arms full and a cereal box under your chin. It doesn't happen only in the supermarket either. Sometimes there's just too much to carry. Here's a solution that'll keep your hands free when you've got an unexpected load.

The pants backpack is an old hobo classic that you'd have used if you were riding boxcars in the 1930s. But there's a lot of life in it yet, and once you've mastered the knack, you'll find plenty of opportunity to use it. The supreme function for the pants backpack is transporting a bundle of dirty clothes to the Laundromat. It's good for family trips to the beach, too. It's obviously best when there's an extra pair of pants around so that you don't leave yourself with cold knees.

What you need:

- one pair of pants
- a belt or similar length of rope
- two lengths of rope or cord (15 inches [38 cm] or so each)

Use the belt/rope as a drawstring to pull through the belt hoops. Bundle up your goods into the top of the trousers and close tightly with the drawstring. Now place the bag with the opening downward onto your back so that the legs can come over your shoulders.

Stuff the trouser ends into the belt loop and wind them around again. This will hold firm but also allow you to make adjustments.

Having the trousers upside down allows you to have the wider, more comfortable part of the leg over your shoulder, but as an alternative you can have the legs coming up from under your armpits and over the top. The great benefit of this is the accessible back pockets, though it's at the expense of a slightly less generous shoulder strap.

EMERGENCY COFFEE DEVICE

Every coffee drinker knows that the best coffee is made by the filter method. And we all know that just because it's an emergency doesn't mean that we need to compromise on standards.

In a crisis when gourmet coffee is called for, here's how a large plastic bottle comes to the rescue.

What you need:

- large, clean plastic bottle
- knife/sharp scissors
- filter papers

1. Put the kettle on.

2. Slice the bottle somewhere below the neck, preferably at the widest part, to make a funnel. Keep in mind that the "bottom" is the main coffee receptacle, so don't make it too small.

3. Place the funnel in the bottom part. If it slips through, slightly twist it so that it jams in place.

4. Put your filter paper into the funnel and add coffee.

5. After the water has boiled, let it stop bubbling and gently pour the required amount onto the coffee.

THE NEWSPAPER BODY WARMER

Stuffing a paper under your coat to keep warm is a piece of urban lore that began with the well-off middle class when caught out in the cold at the races or out riding. I found references to it in two newspapers from the turn of the last century when gentlemen were advised, "an excellent chest protector for a cold day is a folded newspaper buttoned under the overcoat."

Newspaper delivery boys have been using this trick for years: a newspaper down the front to keep out the wind chill and one at the back for extra insulation. For full coverage, a larger-format newspaper is preferred.

In cases of extreme cold, you can make a really big difference by inserting a snug filling of scrunched-up newspaper between the main newspaper and your body or undergarments. Fill in around the entire torso, front and back, to keep your vital organs warm.

THE URBAN ROBINSON CRUSOE TEST
60 MINUTES ON A TRAFFIC ISLAND

In the first few days of his 20 years marooned on a desert island, Robinson Crusoe had to choose what to salvage from the wreck of his ship. He started with rum and tobacco but then got a bit more practical and hauled back all kinds of useful odds and ends. It's

Handy items for island survival:

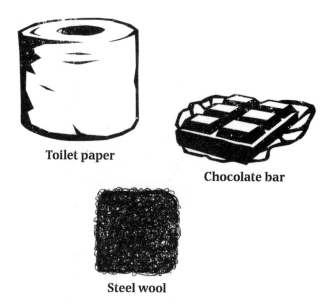

Toilet paper

Chocolate bar

Steel wool

a scenario that's often mimicked in survival courses, where students get a minute to pick the five or ten items they'd salvage from a ship or plane crash.

Well here's the urban bushcraft version. Based on what you've learned through this section of the book, could you pick what you need when the pressure is really on?

Here's the scenario. You've run out of gas, and there's an hour to wait until roadside assistance gets through the traffic to you. What would you buy at the corner store with the five bucks you have? All items must serve genuine survival priorities—fire, shelter, warmth, and so on.

Here's one exemplary set of purchases offering options for starting a fire, warmth, sustenance, and a chance to catch up on the price of your shares or the racing results.

Bar of chocolate	$.50
Soda	$.80
Roll of toilet paper (× 2)	$.60
Newspapers (× 3)	$1.90
Brillo pads (× 10)	$1.00
TOTAL	**$4.80**

BREAK A LOCK WITH A SOCK

Cheap combination locks—you know they aren't a good idea when you buy them, but somehow they draw you in with that seductive offer; use any combination you like, a set of three numbers you'll always remember. Now, what was that combination again?

Breaking a lock apart with a sock when you've forgotten the code is not only a handy way to open it, but also a pretty powerful demonstration of why you should never buy such a lock again.

Here's what to do:
- Remove one sock.
- Slip it through the horseshoe-shaped part of the lock.

- Grab one end of the sock in each hand and give both a sharp tug, pulling away from the lock barrel.
- Try it three or four times.

This is a last-ditch attempt to open a troublesome lock. If it works, then the satisfaction may go some way toward countering the shame you're now feeling at having a lock that can be broken with a sock!

If you want a less brutal way into your lock, try cracking the combination; it's normally pretty easy on a cheap lock. Pull up the horseshoe bar as far as it will go and turn each number wheel until you feel a small click on the bar, or until the wheel is harder to turn. It's as simple as that.

Urban bushcraft through the ages:
ELLSWORTH JAEGER

These days TV channels are full of shows about what they call survival techniques. Their stars have stubbly chins, eat bugs, and wear bandannas. And because this is pretty macho territory, there's a strong whiff of competition about who does it better, who knows the most, and which of them came first. Well guys, you can break that up right now. It's none of you, it's this fellow right here. Step forward please, Mr. Ellsworth Jaeger.

At this point I imagine Ellsworth shuffling forward looking at his shoes. Being in the spotlight is not his scene. He'd much rather be back at the Buffalo Museum of Science, where he was a faculty member during the 1940s. He spent his working life collecting the wisdom of the wilderness and his weekends putting it into practice, in the woods. Ellsworth could tell you ten different ways to build a bed from branches, cook beans in a hole, or pack your goods on your mule. He was a compiler of "Indian lore" as it once was known; the "wildwood wisdom," that came directly from frontiersmen in coonskin hats and the native people who'd taught them.

These "wilderness men of the past" are invoked like gods. But Ellsworth could already smell on the breeze the arrival of a new breed of outdoor enthusiast. "The myriad jungle jangle gadgets of some of our modern outdoorsmen would make our ancestral buckskin men turn in their grave," he writes. This was decades before the first energy bar or Gore-tex jacket, but he could see how things were going. Gadgets were taking over from know-how. And mercifully we have his books as a line in the sand, a record of what went before.

His book, *Wildwood Wisdom,* has been by my constant companion for years. It deals with the basics of life and death in the wilderness but manages still to radiate soothing warmth. You can read *Wildwood Wisdom* like a novel; it's an escape to a land where rivers are clean and a leafy willow branch bed awaits you in the woods. The cozy glow is fueled by his folksy drawings; a raccoon sniffing a corn bake or a chipmunk trying on a ten-gallon hat. My personal favorite shows a bear digging what appears to be a latrine in the woods.

Wildwood Wisdom was written in the final years of World War II. Against a backdrop of mistrust and uncertainty, Pearl Harbor and the Battle of Midway, Ellsworth built a bridge to a dependable world of constant values. Sure, there's a hint of nostalgia in there too, a backward glance to the frontier days of Americans like Daniel Boone or Davy Crockett. But to see that as the joy of these books is to miss the point.

To him the wilderness, his "Wildwood," isn't a hiding place, but a destination. It's comforting and the place he wanted to be. And that's the mark of a true bushman. And that's what he was. I have spoken.

6.
WORKPLACE
STRATEGY

At work we operate under strict rules about what to say, what to do, and when to go home. And whether it's the glint of your cufflinks or the cut of your jeans, the way you look matters, too. Work is now the most formal event in our lives. And it's under constraints like these that our primal urges long to rebel and to show themselves in all their glory.

Ever since childhood, we've learned to obey rules that go against instinct: We put the toilet seat down, use a knife and fork impeccably, and hardly ever spill food on our shirts. So by now, we're pretty good at hiding the urges within. Sitting in a meeting, suited and booted, shaved and deodorized, we play the game of pretending that this is all there is, that our animal appetites are sated with the new business plans, that our life's aim is to see the merger proposal accepted by the head office. And subsequently everyone around the table keeps their primal self buttoned up and reined in. It's there all right, and we know it. It's reliably uncouth, totally unprofessional, and never to be mentioned. It's the 800-pound gorilla in the room.

But the urban bushman refuses to make his inner caveman redundant, preferring to recruit him as a trusty ally to help in the fight against drudgery at a desk, or boredom in the budget hotel. Whether flicking rubber bands across the office or swapping glances in the meeting room, he knows this is where his instincts can reap dividends. By embracing his savage side, the bushman at work can let off steam, make the days fly by, and, when push comes to shove, even get a bit more work done.

IN A MEETING

"I'm sorry I can't talk now, I'm in a meeting . . ."

The business meeting is a fenced-off piece of formality, a ritual that's entirely sacrosanct. Here are a few tips to help the bushman emerge from the meeting room unscathed.

TIMING IS EVERYTHING

The most powerful person in the meeting is the last one to walk in before it starts. The message is that things can only happen once this person is in the room. This is when being late is a privilege of power. The lowest-status person is the one who arrives after it

> **Once upon a time,** showing up for work without a tie and calling your boss by his first name would have gotten you canned. Now it's just the way work is. But don't be deceived. All this apparent informality on the surface doesn't change what goes on beneath it. It's a battle for status, power, and personal gain—in a nutshell, all of the stuff that's worth getting out of bed for.

starts. This is an open statement that their role is unimportant. That person was just plain late.

The village elders of Madagascar and Sir Alan Sugar know all about the privilege of being late. They know how to time their entrance into a meeting. Just like Donald Trump in the show *The Apprentice,* they want to be the last to walk into the room. It shows they hold the power. But in the village there's a problem. There are a lot of elders, and they all want to be the last to arrive. So they've developed a system where instead of arriving late, the meeting is announced two hours early. The villagers arrive on time, and then eventually, the elders show up with the appropriate delay. And finally the chief arrives latest of all and things can start.

STAY STANDING—THE HANNIBAL LECTER TRICK

Have we all seen *The Silence of the Lambs?* Well, you know that part when Jodie Foster as the FBI agent first meets Anthony Hopkins as the scary cannibal? The camera follows as she walks into the dingy prison wing and along a corridor toward his cell. Then the music builds, and we're seeing her point of view, and we know we're about to meet a killer. What happens next is chilling. As he's revealed to us for the first time, Dr. Hannibal Lecter isn't sitting in a corner or lying on his bed, but standing to attention in the middle of his cell, staring straight at her. He knew she was coming, and he's waiting for her. It's the start of a police interview where the criminal is the one who does the questioning. He's the one who's locked up, yet he seems to hold all the cards. And it all starts with his standing up.

I often think about this when I'm in a meeting room being made to wait. Sitting down is a passive submission to a timetable imposed by somebody else. All you can do is wait for him to show up so that things can start. It gives him all of the power. Try staying standing until he arrives, and make him sit first. Things will start when you choose to sit. That way you keep the initiative and, like Hannibal Lecter, take control.

THE POWER OF SILENCE

This is an old classic of the antiques' trader and second-hand car dealer—the urban bushman with an innate expertise in bargaining hard, standing firm, and making the other guy crumble.

The golden rule is to say to yourself: "The next one to speak, loses." Then keep quiet and prove yourself right.

In the creative brainstorming session, the bushman's colleagues yak on in the vain hope of hitting home with one incisive remark. But while his colleagues clamor to fill every available silence with the sound of their voices, the bushman remains aloof, watching from a distance. He sees that silence is the one thing that generates more drivel than anything else, and the thing that every office worker fears the most. So he keeps quiet and turns silence to his own advantage.

This works purely because silence is unnerving. To stay silent is to suggest an inner calm, and that's sure to unnerve any office opponent. The more confident you are in your silence, the more churned up in self-doubt your opponent will become.

Here's how to use it. You're in a frank exchange of views with a colleague. You sense he isn't going to back down. He's convinced he's right. Now ask him a critical question, something related to his professional judgment. Listen to his answer and wait for him to stop. Then hold eye contact and just say nothing. This is where he starts to squirm. Your silence unnerves him so much he begins to babble, and then you've got him. He'll start to show you all the flaws in his argument, dredge up his doubt and indecision, and lay it before you. Anything but silence.

This is also an old favorite in negotiations. Instead of reacting to your counterpart's offer, just say nothing. Pretty soon he'll fill the silence with a lower offer.

GO UNDERCOVER WITHOUT LEAVING YOUR DESK

Leaving your coat on the back of your chair when you slip out early, diverting your office phone to your cell—there are all kinds of ways the bushman can cover his tracks at work.

Here's how the e-mail application on your desktop computer can provide virtual cover, just when you need it most.

I once got a circular e-mail, which was sent to the whole company, asking if anyone had a large bird outfit. More specifically, it had to be a black or brown bird such as a crow or thrush, and definitely not a chicken, robin, or duck. It was a change from the usual stuff about missing staplers, but it demonstrates the depth of a problem the urban bushman confronts every day. Our inboxes are clogged with trivialities. They arrive with a ping and a tempting envelope icon, and then slowly consume our time in little one-minute parcels. But all that changes when you learn to use your inbox to go undercover.

Before e-mail, when people picked up the phone, secretaries and receptionists had to lie to cover their bosses' tracks by making excuses and saying their bosses were out. But now the threat comes by e-mail, and there's no secretary to deflect them. There's a simple solution, however, in this democratic world of new technology. Just switch on your out-of-office assistant.

Think about it. When you send an e-mail and get back an out-of-office message, who suspects for a moment it might not be true? Who wonders whether this is just a cover story—a cunning ploy allowing us to work on something more worthwhile than responding to e-mail? Nobody does, because we believe what our computer tells us. The out-of-office function is the best liar in the office. It would be stupid not to use it.

OFFICE SPYCRAFT: PASSWORD HACKING

Password protecting your e-mail inbox is a fundamental rule of office life, so the bushman can't resist the challenge of guessing the various passwords of everyone in the office. Not because he wants to get into their inboxes and send obscene messages to the CEO. Of course not! This classic piece of spycraft is dignified with a far more gentlemanly outcome.

Here's how:

1. Pick your target and begin observation. You need to be standing near him as he logs in. Pick out single letters and numbers as he types, one or two per day. Start at the very beginning or the very end of the password sequence. This is easier for touch typists, but we all have a fairly good understanding of what's where on the keyboard.

2. Log your observations, noting if you can, where each keystroke comes in the order.

3. Listen to the rhythm and tap it out on a keyboard, counting the number of keystrokes made. Once your list has nearly enough characters, start trying to crack the code. Think of it as an anagram and find a likely word, such as the name of your target's child, hometown, or pet.

Try out the options on another computer (one that allows you to log in twice) or on your target's computer when he's not around.

It shouldn't take long before you crack it. Well done! Now that you have the password, here's what to do. It just wouldn't be right not to inform your colleague that his secret is out. Design a calling card and leave it on his desk to let him know he's been anonymously hacked. But it also gives you the upper hand. Though you didn't read any of his private files, he won't know that, and there can be nothing more unnerving.

Set yourself the target of cracking the target password within two weeks, or ten days, of observation. Canadian spy instructors who worked on this system reckon on needing nine days to crack a password.

PASSWORDS FOR PLEBS

Two recent surveys, one in America and one in Britain, show that the thought process leading to an easy-to-hack password is startlingly similar—no matter which side of the Atlantic you're on. And, apparently, true simpletons everywhere have a curious attraction to typing the word "monkey."

AMERICA'S MOST POPULAR PASSWORDS	BRITAIN'S MOST POPULAR PASSWORDS
password	123
123456	password
qwerty	Liverpool
abc123	letmein
letmein	123456
monkey	qwerty
myspace1	Charlie
password1	monkey
Blink182	Arsenal
(Your first name)	Thomas

OFFICE WARFARE

To some it's a juvenile distraction; to others it's a way to give the warrior inside a workout without having to join your colleagues sweating their lunch hour away in a kickboxing class.

Ever since he first slung a jacket on the back of his swivel chair and played around with the lever under the seat, working man has been looking for a way to relax at work. If only he could quickly tune out and rediscover what life is all about, then he'd get back to the sales figures like never before.

From cigarette break to coffee break, he's tried a number of different things. Stress balls and executive toys worked for awhile, but too much staring at a Newton's Cradle can lead into some dark and dangerous places. Then came team-building breaks and water-cooler moments, but getting cozy and communal with his colleagues wasn't really what he had in mind.

But by using the resources of the office environment to revive man's primal purpose, urban bushcraft has hit on the perfect formula for a happy workforce. With nothing but a few office booby traps and a pocketful of rubber bands, he's perfectly equipped to get through the 9–5 with a spring in his step.

STEALTH GUN WITH A HIGHLIGHTER PEN

The slippery top of those fat office highlighter pens allows a unique opportunity to fire, seemingly by accident. As illustrated, all you need is a pen and a strong document clip.

Here's how to do it:

- Take the lid off the highlighter and squeeze the sides together a bit. Now fix the clip to the lid, slightly off-center.
- Lightly put the lid back on the pen, but don't push it down.
- Adopt an innocent and uncaring expression, and hold it.
- When you're ready to fire, point the clip handles toward the target and press the lid down firmly onto the pen. The slight flexibility of the lid means it will expand, forcing the clip to fly off in your chosen direction. You, of course, will appear oblivious.

RUBBER BANDS: SOME ADVANCED AERODYNAMICS

When an office bushman worthy of the name spends his career near a stationery cupboard stocked with boxes of rubber bands, the result is something truly extraordinary.

Flicking rubber bands off the end of your thumb is fine for the classroom, but with this technique, rubber-band aerodynamics rise to the level of the boardroom.

With a simple adjustment to firing technique, the rubber band is turned from a uselessly floppy projectile into an aerodynamic miracle with swerve, lift, and a rather marvelous swooshing sound as it hits your colleague's ear.

THE TECHNIQUE

A large rubber band is all you need.

Here's how to do it:

1. Hook the band over the index finger of your lead hand (for me it's the left) and pull it back by hooking it with the middle finger of your rear hand (my right).

2. When it's stretched fairly tight, put your thumb up through the hoop and pull the band back farther still with your thumb instead of the finger that you now need to take out of the way. This switch pulls the band in a different direction, slightly to one side. That's what's meant to happen. One side of the band (the left) is now much tighter than the other.

3. Hold steady and take aim by lining up your thumb and the front finger, like a gun. The band will fly in a curve to the right (away from the tighter side), so aim to the left of the target.

4. Fire by gently lowering the thumb and watch your band swerve as it flies. Listen for that swoosh. Once your colleagues get to know that sound, it will strike fear in their hearts, earning you their undying respect and giving you the edge in any skirmish.

Now practice and practice some more. Pretty soon you'll be able to predict and adjust the swerve, and hit targets around corners.

How it works

The secret of this technique is in the lopsided pullback, making one side stretch more than the other, so that on release it spins in flight. The spinning band forms a flat disk with uncanny aerodynamic properties. It has a curved path that's predictable enough to allow for extreme accuracy, and the extra lift produces a flight with 50–70 percent more range than a standard flick.

Plausible deniability

One of many great things about curved flight is that the band hits its target from a direction that rules you out as a suspect. And since there's no gun or launcher, there's no evidence to pin it on you. You have plausible deniability.

RUBBER BANDS—A REFRESHER

In the event of office warfare, you may need a refresher on the correct way to fire a rubber band. It's been a few years since school, after all. As all schoolboys know, there are one- and two-handed techniques, both imitating a gun to allow you to roam the office firing at will.

THE HANDGUN

Here's how to make it:

- Load the band by wrapping it around the tip of the little finger, which is curled toward the base of the thumb.
- Stretch the other end of the band behind the thumb and hook it over the extended index finger. Your handgun is now loaded.
- To fire, gently release the little finger.

This is especially suitable for the short, thicker rubber bands, used to tie bundles of asparagus.

THE SEMI-AUTOMATIC

Here the band is held by the vertical thumb of the front hand while the other end is gripped between thumb and first finger of the rear "trigger" hand, which pulls back for maximum tension before releasing. This is more suitable for a longer rubber band.

THE OFFICE TRAPPER

Lying in wait for a victim to blunder into our trap is a pleasure that runs deep in our DNA, from the Sumatran pig hunter setting his pitfall trap to the schoolboy balancing a cup of water over the classroom door. And the workplace is the ideal environment to reconnect with the trapper within.

For primitive man, traps saved on hours of running around with a spear and allowed him a rare sit-down. Hunting like this had it all: There was the careful construction, the tense anticipation, and then the eventual satisfaction of a job well done. But best of all, trapping made him feel clever. It's a game of chess we've been playing for thousands of years, against some pretty dumb opponents, and, not surprisingly, we've grown to like it.

In the old days, trap design was passed down from father to son, over generations. Now things move a bit faster, and they're passed around in seconds over the Internet. Given that half the planet seems to work in an office, there's a rich culture to draw on, and you have every chance of finding the ideal trap for the particular challenges of your office.

Plentiful free materials and lots of spare time make the perfect conditions in which to develop your skills as a virtuoso of desktop defense gadgets. This one is a bit tricky to make, but the principle is simple enough. Make your own modifications as you go along, and if it works, go with it.

The builders and designers of OfficeGuns.com and Instructables.com are working hard to keep office weaponry and trapping alive. I'm grateful to them for their inspiration and for showing me I'm not alone.

A NOTE ON PREY

Usually, in the average workplace, there's no shortage of victims to choose from. This is a place where squabbles over territory escalate into open war, where persistent offenses like stealing a newspaper from your desk or hogging the photocopier can fuel a ravenous hunger for revenge.

But choose your prey carefully. The wise bushman prefers to rise above everyday quarrels, preferring not to give away his presence by targeting obvious rivals. Instead he moves around unseen, picking the most demanding of challenges in the knowledge that, to the hunter, the real thrill is always in the chase.

THE HOT DESK MOUSETRAP

When sharing desks gets to be too much, don't lock your computer, booby trap it.

This is a pretty simple device to get you going, powered by a domestic mousetrap, and sprung by any tiny movement on the computer mouse. It's designed to encourage the colleague using your desk to find an alternative place to spend a few hours on Facebook.

Once the trap is set, it means that as soon as your colleague moves that mouse, a shower of your choice* will rain down on a

---

* A small amount of water (from the water cooler, of course) works well, if you're prepared for the desk to get wet. Otherwise, a pot of glitter gets the message across, with the added benefit of a wider "footprint."

wide area within a couple of feet or so of the monitor. The great thing about it is that the trigger mechanism can stay completely out of sight.

What you need:

- Coat hanger
- Mousetrap
- A film canister or cup (if firing water)
- Duct tape
- Pliers
- Fishing line
- Water/glitter

What to do:

- First, find a level platform behind your monitor where you can fix the trap.
- Now use the wire from the coat hanger to extend the arms of the mousetrap to reach over the top of the monitor.

This has the added benefit of giving your chosen projectile more velocity.

- Tape the film canister, paper cup, or other small receptacle to the end of the new arm you've just made.
- Fix a length of fishing line to the trigger bit (where the mouse nibbles the cheese) so that any slight tug will spring the trap.
- Firmly secure with tape the whole assembly to the back of the monitor, or just behind it. It needs to be horizontal and on a steady base.
- Thread the length of wire or fishing line discreetly behind the monitor and attach it to the mouse cable, out of sight.
- Now set the trap (extremely carefully) and retreat. Oh, and as most people discover when they do this the first time, don't fill anything with water until the very end.

Warning: Range finding is a big issue with this trap, but that can be assessed on a trial run with just a few ripped shreds of paper in the canister.

As soon as the trap is sprung, you make yourself a highly prized target for a similar trap. Trust me, I know from experience.

PEN BOW AND ARROW

There's a time when every hunter has to give up trapping and stalk his prey instead. This pen bow and arrow is his weapon of choice.

Here's what to do:

1. Raid the stationery cabinet for a pen with a slightly flexible body and a rubber band that can just loop around it lengthways.

2. Take the pen apart and use a small crosshead screwdriver (Phillips type), or anything spiked, to prod a hole in the middle. The hole must be just big enough to push the nib holder through. If you're using a hard plastic pen, you'll struggle to get a hole through it without it shattering.

3. Hook the rubber band around the pen body, insert your arrow, pull back, and take aim.

The best use for this potentially harmful weapon is in the controlled environment of an office shooting range. Most important of all, don't point or fire it toward anybody's face.

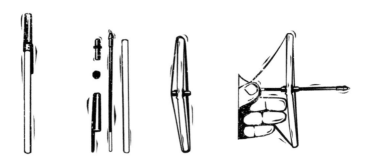

THE BOREDOM OF THE BUSINESS TRAVELER

One thing and one thing alone can ease the tedium of the drab business hotel. When the walls start closing in, cooking on the built-in appliances is a tonic for the soul. Most of the stuff you need can be bought at a local store or picked up for free around the hotel. Put the do-not-disturb sign on the door, and start cooking.

THE HOTEL-ROOM CHEF

You're staying in a hotel designed for corporate travelers. The deli closed half an hour ago, and a room service club sandwich is the price of dinner for two at your local restaurant. You could go out, of course, but that would mean mingling with your fellow colleagues, when all you really want to do is to take off your name badge and reclaim your feral identity. It's time to get cooking with your hotel-room appliances.

Look around the room; it's stuffed with gadgets, and every one of them can be turned into a cooker. I'm just going to start you off with a few of my old favorites; once your bushman brain gets into gear, I've no doubt you'll be inventing plenty more. After all, food is a great incentive.

Of course, all of these methods can be used elsewhere; it's just that I know how soul destroying these hotel bedrooms can be. Take care not to cause any damage, but don't worry about the mess: The maids have seen far worse.

THE HOTEL COOK'S TOOLBOX

Keep your cooking gear in a spare bag ready to drop into your luggage in a second. If you're going on a flight, check security and restrictions.

Your hotel cooking gear:

- Aluminum foil—several long sheets
- Wire strippers
- A small metal grill (optional)
- Instant noodles
- Shrink-wrapped hot dogs/pancakes/burritos
- Maple syrup

Once in the hotel take any chance to pocket sachets of condiments and seasoning, and borrow some cutlery from the dining room as soon as you check in. Don't feel bad—you've paid for it.

Cooking hot dogs by electrocution is a staple of American culture. In the 1960s it was a standard science experiment in school, and at home, the Presto Hot Dogger was a familiar gadget. The whole family could watch as 120 volts passed through the writhing, steaming hot dogs, accompanied by electric sizzling and the smell of burning flesh. "Cooks 12 hot dogs in 60 seconds," boasted the TV ads.

THE 100-WATT HOT DOG

The plain old bedside lamp is a good place to start. Before long, by the magical properties of the discovery of Messrs. Ohm, Faraday, and Edison, you'll be tucking into the quickest hot dogs you've ever eaten.

What you need:

- A lamp or light fitting
- Wire cutters/blade
- Prepacked hot dogs
- Ketchup/mustard and bread (optional)

Warning: If you can change a lightbulb and wire a plug, then you're probably qualified to carry out the electrical rewiring this job requires. Just be sure not to touch any bare wires or the "live" hot dog when the plug is switched on.

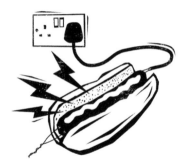

All you're doing really is plugging in your hot dog and allowing electricity to fry it from the inside. The current of 120 volts allows for a nice slow cooking time, which is good for flavor.

There are two options for wiring up your hot dog. You can take the ends of the cable out of the lamp and use them as your cooking "prongs," then just rewire the lamp after use. Or, if there's a lot of spare flex, you may get away with slightly adjusting it by cutting it near the plug and once you've eaten, simply rewiring the plug. Remember to remove the scrap piece of flex in case it arouses suspicion.

What to do:

- Unplug lamp and switch off plug.
- Prepare a bare end of cable by stripping the plastic insulation from the two wires inside to give you an exposed section that's just longer than your hot dog. Stick both wires lengthwise into the hot dog and wrap them together where they stick out of the other end.
- Now just plug in. Don't touch the hot dog or wires!
- Switch on the power and allow a few seconds to cook.
- Unplug the lamp, remove your hot dog, and place it in the bun.

For a slower-cooked hot dog, strip just a few centimeters of each cable and put one into each end of the hot dog. This will take 2–3 minutes to cook through.

Cut out and leave any black or charred parts of the hot dog—they may contain nasty deposits from the wires.

TIPS

- Pierce the hot dog so that it doesn't explode if it gets too hot.
- Blistering of the skin is a sign it's cooked.
- If you have pickles (always advisable if you're eating hot dogs), try passing a current through them and watch them glow.

LIGHTBULB TOAST

The incandescent lightbulb with its glowing filament converts just 15 percent of the power it uses into light. The good thing about this scandalous inefficiency is that the rest is released as heat, which means that if you're using old-fashioned lightbulbs, you may as well cook on them.

First, find the most powerful bulb in the room. You need to suspend your raw bread above the light, so up-lighters and wall lights are ideal; all you need is something across the top to act as a grill. You can improvise, but I carry one with me, because whatever you use will get marked.

Lining the inside of the shade with foil will help reflect more heat onto your toast, and it will catch the crumbs, too.

With a 60-watt bulb, allow a minute per side of bread, but it all really depends on how brown you like your toast.

The surface temperature of a 100-watt bulb can reach 390°-500°F (200°-260°C), so don't touch!

THE IRON CHEF

A hot iron is a precision tool that allows the application of intense heat to small areas, so it's perfect for searing meat and seafood. You'll be surprised how effective this is.

The best iron to use is the most basic model, with an entirely flat bottom and no holes, which is fortunate as they're still pretty common in hotels. If you can't find the iron, it's usually in the closet with the laundry bags and that thing for shining your shoes.

If you're using a multi-functional modern iron with holes for steam, be extra careful to seal the food by wrapping it in foil or grease will get into the reservoir and your collars will forever smell of bacon.

Iron-chef's bacon and eggs

This great breakfast uses the iron in both its cooking modes. For the bacon you need an ironing surface (put a towel onto the ironing board in case of greasy leaks), and for the eggs, fix the iron upside down so that you can use it as a hot plate. With some models, you can use the handle as a clip that slides under the ironing board or a table, holding it in place to create a ready-made warming oven.

What you need:
- Bacon, cut into thin slices
- Two eggs, whisked (use a plastic fork from the restaurant)
- Tinfoil—about two 6-inch (15 cm) squares
- A tinfoil "boat" made out of double-thickness foil, about the size of the iron's hot surface (this is going to be your cooking "pan")
- A dash of milk (two mini-servings from the tea and coffee basket will do)

What to do:
1. Heat the iron all the way up to cotton/linen. If there is a steam setting, switch it off!
2. Put the bacon pieces between the two squares of foil and crimp the edges so that it makes a loose bag around the bacon.

3. Press the iron onto the bacon in bursts of 20 seconds, opening one side of the foil packet every few minutes to check and allow steam to escape. Slightly crisp bacon takes about 10 minutes of ironing.
4. Put the bacon to one side.
5. Now grease inside your foil "boat" with some of the bacon fat and place it on top of the propped-up iron.
6. Mix the milk with the eggs and pour the mixture into the boat. As the mix begins to thicken, stir or shake to make a rough omelet.
7. After about 7 minutes, add the bacon, and warm it through for another minute.
8. Serve with coffee (made the normal way in the coffeemaker).

Iron-pressed sandwiches

The iron is really a one-sided sandwich toaster, which means a grilled-cheese sandwich or a quesadilla are perfect hotel-room snacks. Wrap your sandwich in tinfoil (single thickness) and press with a hot iron for several minutes on each side. It's a good idea to spread a bit of mayonnaise onto the outside surface of the sandwich if you can—it helps it to brown.

Iron-seared scallops

Season the scallops. (You did get some packets of salt and pepper from the restaurant, didn't you?) Put them between two sheets of foil, and press the iron down onto the foil for 1–2 minutes per side. Shrimp is a good alternative. Make sure whatever seafood you use is cooked through properly.

THE COFFEEMAKER

The filter coffeemaker looks like a versatile tool for cooking. But there are drawbacks: It takes a lot of cleaning. Even then it can be hard to get rid of the coffee residue, and that's going to spoil those delicate flavors. I prefer to keep it simple and save the showy stuff for the other appliances. Even so, it can provide some useful accompaniments to the main event.

The pot

Cook in the hot water that drips through into the pot, adding your ingredients before it fills up. It's plenty warm enough to cook things like instant oatmeal, noodles, or a boiled egg.

The basket

The filter basket makes an effective vegetable steamer. Put broccoli or finely chopped carrots into the basket and run water through the machine until your veggies are ready.

Sauces

The best way to make a sauce is in the pot. Remove the filter basket for easy access and then mix up a roux with butter and flour, gently stirring in milk and seasoning for a simple white sauce. I prefer to use the coffeemaker for sweet sauces to go with a dessert. The hot plate's gentle heat is just right for melting chocolate into cream, and this way, if the coffee flavor lingers, so what? Just call it mocha.

Some people will try to convince you that you can use a coffeemaker as a kind of automatic sauce maker, putting cream and lemon into the boiler, filtering it over some herbs in the basket, and letting it reduce over the hot plate into a rich goo. It's ambitious, and tempting to try it in the name of science. But, please don't. It will kill the coffeemaker, and your culinary ambitions with it.

THE TROUSER PRESS

It's come through some tough times, and it's been the butt of countless jokes, but the trouser press has endured it all with dignity. Its tireless dedication to one simple idea deserves all of our respect, no matter how crumpled our trousers may be.

It started out in the 1930s as the "valet stand," a glorified coat hanger, and the Corby trouser press evolved from there. Then came the 1960s, and the trouser press went electric (four years before Dylan—take that hippies!). Now, at last, the traveling salesman was free of crumpled trouser anxiety, all thanks to Corby's pin-sharp creases. The trouser press had a perfect solution for a genuine need and became the constant ally of the highway and Travelodge fraternity from that day on.

But times changed. By the 1970s crumpled trousers were cool and the trouser press embodied everything that wasn't. But the trouser press stubbornly clung to that hotel-room wall; because hoteliers know deep down, that we love it. Like a secular Gideon's Bible, it belongs in our hotel rooms, and whether you need it or not, it just feels good to know it's there.

Any trouser press is suitable for cooking, but look for models with variable temperature control and timer settings up to 45 minutes. The heat setting on most presses allows for a top cooking temperature of 60°–80°F (15°–27°C). The Corby 7700 is typical in hotels, and has all the features you'll need.

The trouser-press pancake party

The shape and size of the trouser press make it perfect for party food—pancakes, chapattis, burritos, or whatever you call them. Better still, they come in precooked packs ready to be warmed through and served.

Wrap pancakes in foil and heat for five minutes in a trouser press set to around 60. Prepare a few fillings in advance or see what you can scavenge from around the hotel.

You can fit in about five 8-inch (20 cm) pancakes at a time. If you warm them in advance, keep up to 15 pancakes in there in small stacks of three on a low heat setting. Or load a few in the press each morning, flip the switch when you get back to the room, and have piping hot pancakes ready in the few minutes it takes to hop into the shower.

Grilled Eggplant à la Corby

- Thinly sliced eggplant (about 5mm)
- Foil
- Oil and seasoning

Put the eggplant slices in foil with a good dash of olive oil and cook for a full 45-minute cycle at 60°–70°F (15°–21°C).

DIY Room Service

Menu (Half Board)

Breakfast

Coffeemaker oatmeal

*Iron-cooked bacon and eggs served with
lightbulb toast*

Tea/coffee

Dinner

Iron-seared scallops

Coffeemaker noodles with herb and lemon sauce

Slow-grilled eggplant à la trouser press

Coffeemaker-steamed broccoli florets

7.
PURELY FOR PLEASURE

The urban bushman never lets up on his quest for adventure, even on the weekend. Rather than zoning out while mowing the lawn or fine-tuning the catalog of his DVD collection, he turns to the pursuit of a special brand of bushcraft that's purely for pleasure.

As a kid I could shoot straight, fly a plane, and punch a man with a satisfying ker-thwack—at least until I was called in for dinner. As I got older, and dinnertime got later, the fantasies grew ever more grandiose. Throughout our boyhood we play at being adults in the world of adults, with an all-access pass to the limitless universe of possibilities.

Then we grow up. But it doesn't feel as if we've grown up at all. It feels more as if we've stayed the same while the world around us got boring. Our toys are up in the attic, we're on the bus to work, and our shaving rash stings like hell. Needless to say that all-access pass never materializes either. This is the universal experience of the male human.

With a bit of guidance, the urban bushman can bring playtime back into everyday life, turning his curiosity and inventiveness toward a search for grown-up kicks—the kind that can be had when using bees as an aid to urban navigation or when on an archaeological exploration down the back of the sofa. The mission is to bring back that old exuberance as we roll around in the mud and the minutiae of urban life, just for the fun of it.

ARMCHAIR ARCHAEOLOGY

The TV remote control, $3.73 in small change, an olive from last week's pizza—all end up at the back of the sofa. So why not enlist the whole household for an afternoon of systematic soft furnishings excavation, and create an archaeological timeline of the past few years in your living room?

This is a well-organized dig. Each person takes an armchair or sofa and begins the painstaking process of sifting and searching, dating and recording, as artifacts are uncovered and history is revealed. Build your own record of key events in the recent past as you turn up a Smartie from the top of last year's birthday cake, Grannie's reading glasses, and a small army of Star Wars figurines, orange peels, and bits of walnut shell (from the Christmas before last, I presume).

To create your final display, lay out all of the finds on a length of paper (toilet paper works well) with key dates marked along a timeline. Particularly prized finds are old coins, missing pieces of jigsaw puzzles, and cards.

THE SIDEWALK GARDENER

Gardening doesn't have to be all about perfectly trimmed edges, gardening gloves, and sprinklers. The urban bushman goes in search of his horticultural nirvana with some extreme gardening as he prepares to take on one of the most hostile terrains of the city environment and tame it.

Hearty herb

Herbs are tough little street fighters that can eke out a living in the meanest of streets. If you ask any gardener, they'll back me up; they're always recommending herbs for the cracks in the crazy paving, so what's the difference? Let's grow a sidewalk herb garden.

The herbs that work best are the woodier ones (thyme, marjoram, oregano). They like gritty soil, so the gaps between the paving stones are just right—it reminds them of the alpine nooks and crannies of home on the mountains.

Start out with a few favorites outside the front door and be the first to turn the pavement into an overflow herb garden. Some of the herbs will go into the pot; others will release their fragrance as you pass and crush scented leaves underfoot.

Next you can start to cultivate a colony or two on some more distant parts of your daily route—outside the train station or beside the bus stop. Places where paving has been recently removed for cable laying or pipe maintenance are particularly fertile, as are stretches habituated by dog walkers.

DEATH TO THE BARBECUE

Put down those tongs and step away from the barbecue. You've got bigger things on your mind.

For urban man the sight of food browning over the embers is a repeat showing of his finest hour, a reminder of how he controlled one of nature's most terrifying forces and how it made him feel like king. So it makes sense that where there's a barbecue, there's always a man presiding over the burst sausages, and he won't surrender those tongs without a struggle. This polite little ritual of hot dogs and hamburgers is as close as he gets these days to satisfying his primal need. But why settle for this substitute when you can have the real thing?

When man cooks, he wants people to take notice. He wants flames, and he wants to leave great big scorch marks on the earth. Get ready for the Chicken Inferno!

CHICKEN INFERNO

A golden brown rotisserie chicken, ready in 15 minutes of blazing glory!

Cooking in unusual ways on unconventional ovens is one method to turn food preparation into an adventure with man appeal. The other way is to make it big and make it spectacular, because when a man cooks, he instinctively wants people to take notice.

This chicken recipe is my once-a-year dose of adrenaline cooking that has the right mix of mischief and theater to keep me going until the following summer. It's particularly effective after dark.

What you need:

- A bale of hay/straw, tinder dry
- A cleaned metal canister/drum, about 5–8 gallons (20–30 liters)*
- A clean, large bottle
- One chicken

---

* A catering-sized cooking-oil drum would be perfect.

- Marinade ingredients
- A large fireproof dish
- Oven gloves

How it works

Your chicken is going to be flash roasted in the center of an inferno of hay.

For ten minutes or so, you'll have a roaring fire to gaze at, and five minutes later, you'll be serving a beautifully cooked chicken to some pretty impressed guests.

Preparation

With a sharp knife, gently score the chicken down to the bone, in half-inch (2-cm) strips so that it all cooks evenly. Now marinade it for at least two hours in a spicy barbecue blend, rubbing the oily mixture in well.

While the chicken's marinating, clean the canister thoroughly and cut off one end with a hacksaw or angle grinder.

Now find an open space where you can safely set light to your mini-haystack, and prepare your guests for the big moment.

Instructions

1. Put the neck of the bottle into the chicken cavity so that the chicken perches on the neck and the bottle. Stand the bottle on the dish to collect the gravy. Gently place the canister over the chicken so that it doesn't touch, and

cover the whole thing with hay in a pyramid shape to make a tightly pressed mini-haystack.

2. Fifteen minutes before you want to serve, light the hay and stand back!

3. Let the fire burn naturally and listen for the chicken sizzling inside. Leave the embers to continue on cooking the bird after the flames have died down.

4. Once the embers have died, brush away the ashes without disturbing the canister. Maybe put a big stone on top to stop it from moving while you clear the hay.

5. Carefully lift off the canister (it will still be very hot) to reveal your roast chicken and delicious bowl of gravy.

As with any roast chicken, prod the meatiest part with a skewer to make sure it's cooked all the way through. If the juices don't run clear, give it another five-minute blast. Your guests are unlikely to object.

MUSSEL MEN

The barbecue is the suburban man's great caveman moment. But it pales beside the pumped-up outdoor cooking that men get away with all over the world. A few summers ago in a corner of France where mussels are big business, I was asked along to a "fête" with a barbecue in the square. When I got there, five or six men were prodding a bonfire with pitchforks, arranging the blazing logs into a base onto which went a cooking pot the size of a cattle trough. Next, a truckload of mussels arrived, to be transferred to the pot by wheelbarrow. The final ingredient was a bathtub of tomato sauce, all stirred by a spade.

That's what I call man-sized catering. The approach was the same as if they'd been putting up a marquee or towing a tractor out of a ditch: There was a job to be done. This wasn't about pretensions to haute cuisine; it was a celebration of the untamed delights of good food and full bellies. When the mussels were served, nobody was commenting on the presentation or quibbling about the seasoning. Food like this demands to be devoured, and it was. I'll take one night like that over any number of summer evenings prodding charcoal.

NAVIGATING WITH CITY BEES

Navigating without a map is a bushcraft perennial, but it's not often you get the chance to recruit an insect to help do away with the A–Z. All you need is a bit of help from a local beekeeper, and you're on your way. First came GPS, and now here's BeePS.

Bees and beekeepers are no strangers to the city, and producing urban honey is the new hobby to have.* This happy fact allows the urban bushman to borrow a technique from the honey hunters of the rainforest and turn it into one of the most adventurous days out the suburbs can offer.

In the jungle, honey is a rare delicacy and the sweet-toothed

---

* Urban honey bees produce more honey than rural bees and seem to be unaffected by environmental pollution. Some producers claim urban honey is more pure because pollen from city gardens hasn't been sprayed with pesticides.

tribesmen have become experts in pinpointing beehives. The simple principle is to catch bees, then release them, and follow them back to the hive. It can be as simple as that, but bees are hard to follow, so you may end up with terrible eyestrain and very little chance of honey. Consequently, the tribesmen do something very clever—a bit of basic triangulation. This is the system now removed from the primary rainforest and reinvented for the urban conurbation.

THE BASIC IDEA

The system works best with three or more people. One of you has to collect the bees and deliver them to the others, who have each picked a different spot within a three-mile radius of the hive. Each participant will then have a container housing a few bees but no idea where the hive is located. Their challenge is to use the bees to guide them in, and the first one to the hive is the winner.

In my ideal world, this sort of thing would be a basic entry test for the army: Here are your bees; now find your way back to base.

What you need:

- **Bees**—for each person, in a suitable container.
  Try asking your friendly beekeeper to do this part.
- **A picnic**—come on, make a day of it.

How it works

Bees are great navigators and can find their hive from anywhere within a 3-mile (5 km) radius. They tend to fly up in a circling motion, and as soon as they have a fix on where they are, they make a "beeline" for home. They navigate by using the angle of the sun, but they're also thought to spot familiar landmarks like highways and big buildings, so look out for appropriate sights around your chosen start point.

To find the hive, first release one bee, watch it closely, and take a rough bearing on its eventual direction (toward the tower block, to the left of the gas station, that sort of thing). Now imagine a line at roughly 90 degrees to the bee's direction and pick a spot about half a mile (a kilometer) away on that line. That's where you should release your next bee. Then repeat the process once more.

WARNING: If there's any possibility that you may have an allergy to bee stings, this is not for you.

SIR FRANCIS GALTON'S SEASIDE SNOOZE PIT

A day at the beach is as close as many of us ever get to a wilderness adventure. As the leader of the expedition, we're called on to make a series of decisions from the start: how much gear to transport (whether to leave the windbreaker in the car), selecting a route (across the dunes or via the firm wet stuff near the sea), and finding a suitable spot to camp. Should it be close to the ice cream vans and crowds or that patch of space near the point?

In the interest of morale, a bit of give and take is inevitable; this is the burden of all expedition leaders. But the urban bushman consoles himself with a pet project on which compromise is totally out of the question—digging his personal snooze pit.

As the leader of several scientific forays across Africa, Victorian explorer and polymath Sir Francis Galton was familiar with the pressure on an expedition leader and understood the need for comfortable rest. When it came to preparing the ground on which he would sleep, Galton spoke from bitter experience when he wrote, "It is disagreeable enough to lie on a perfectly level surface like that of a floor, but the acme of discomfort is to lie upon a convexity." Ah, Sir Francis, you're so right.

By convexity he meant a bump, of course. And nobody likes to sleep on a bump. But it's the next step that's crucial. Instead of a convexity, you hollow out a human-shaped dip, or in Galton's language, a concavity.

The important thing here is to remember that humans aren't flat sided. Imagine the shape of the dip in your mattress when you're asleep, and replicate that in the sand.

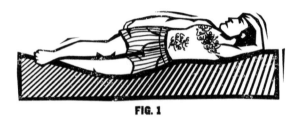

FIG. 1

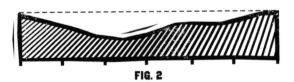

FIG. 2

Preparing a seaside snooze pit (adapted from Sir Francis Galton's The Art of Travel)

1. Remove any stones or other debris.

2. Scrape a hollow, deepest at the point of the hips and accommodating the shoulders.

3. Lay your rug or mat in it.

4. Lie on top of the rug so that your hips and shoulders fit the contours.

5. Commence snoozing.

This project appeals to the obsessive mind of the urban bushman; it takes several tries to get it right, and there's always room for improvement. Galton, of course, took this incredibly seriously and included a calculation of the perfect shape of a sleeping "lair." For a 6-foot-tall man, he calculated that the perfect "concavity" should be 6 inches (15 cm) at its deepest and of the shape shown in the diagram.

Urban bushcraft through the ages: John Steinbeck

Steinbeck had worked as a farmhand, a war correspondent, and a handyman at a ski resort before he wrote *The Grapes of Wrath*, won the Pulitzer Prize, and became a full-time literary icon. But to me his great legacy is the art form he created in a few hours of down time in 1960.

This was the year he decided to tour the country in a camper van with his poodle Charlie. A few months into it, Steinbeck wanted a break, so he booked a hotel while Charlie went to a poodle parlor (all true, I swear). Anyway, he showed up before his room was ready but there was another one available; even though that one hadn't been cleaned, Steinbeck took it while he waited.

To most of us this would have been an unpleasant hour in a dirty hotel room, tiptoeing around somebody else's leavings. Yuk. But Steinbeck didn't see it like that. He tuned into something profound. Looking around the room at the fragments of its previous occupant's life, he felt a natural instinct take over. He was receiving a primal signal, picking up an image of the man who'd been there a few hours before.

The legendary trackers of the Wild West could paint detailed pictures of their quarry by looking at a few broken twigs and some half-covered tracks. Now Steinbeck was carrying on where they left off, reacting to the clues he could read as an urban tracker: an empty whiskey bottle, a few receipts, an unfinished letter in the trash. He built an entire profile of the guest and his previous 24 hours and even gave the guy a name. "As I sat in this unmade room, Lonesome Harry began to take shape and dimension," he wrote later.

We do this all the time—judge people by the space they inhabit. And we expect others to do the same in relation to us. We straighten out our desk or our bedroom before a visitor calls; we leave the right books on show and hide the wrong ones. Steinbeck recognized this innate awareness and gave it dignity. Urban tracking had found its voice. Not bad for a few hours in a dirty hotel room.

120: THE SECRET TO CELL PHONE HAPPINESS

The urban bushman is a primate who uses a cell phone and shares 96 percent of his genetic material with apes who don't. Although our cousins are behind on texting and speed dial, they can show us the perfect number of contacts to store in our phones.

You're on the train and bored with your book. What do you do? Instead of switching on your brain, you get out your phone for some idle flicking through the functions. You browse through the names stored in the memory, either looking for someone to call or weeding out any who deserve to be deleted, then erasing them with satisfaction.

I know I'm not the only one who grooms the contacts in my phone like this. The list represents our unique social network, and we're the hub. Nobody else has a list like it, so it's natural that we're taken with it and enjoy the occasional stroll in its company. But that cozy feeling is hiding some serious science.

120 IS PLENTY

Anthropologists spotted long ago that primitive settlements of people don't grow a lot bigger than 120, and when they do, they split apart. Just as 120 was the upper limit for tight-knit communities in Neolithic settlements long ago, so it is in the villages of developing countries today.

How many weddings have you been to when the guests numbered around 120? How many business conferences hand out roughly that many name badges? When you start looking, the figure 120 is everywhere. It's a well-filled village hall, a packed restaurant; in other words, we seem to know that 120 is just enough.

And apart from weddings and business meetings, there's another place where the spirit of the primitive village lives on: in our phones, of course. If you've held back so far, don't wait any longer. Count the number of contacts stored in your cell, and there's a good chance you'll get to around 120. If you're over, I bet there are a few you could delete without ever missing them.

PRIMATES AND 150

But surely there's no harm in letting our contact list grow and grow, you may say. This is where the apes come in, and here to introduce them is Robin Dunbar, an Oxford anthropologist.

Dunbar studies social circles in apes. And he tells us that if you're in an ape clique, you get groomed on a regular basis; if you aren't, you don't. He noticed that the number of apes in any social circle was always pretty similar. Then he had his big idea: What if

> **I was taught at school** that the basic unit that built the Roman Army was a century—100 men. But that was only after the reforms of Marius in about 100 B.C. Before then, in its heyday, the Roman Army had something else instead: the maniple, a fighting unit of 120–130 men.

the thing that limits the number of social contacts is brain space? To Dunbar it was obvious. To form any meaningful bond, one primate needs to know another primate's entire background, how he fits in, and whom else he's connected with. That's a lot of data to cram into a brain the size of a grapefruit.

Like all anthropologists, Dunbar was keen to point out that we're apes and that we go in for grooming, too. Apes take it literally, squishing the ticks and fleas in each other's fur. We find other ways to get close to each other, like offering rides, sharing meals, or going to movies. And the number of people we allow to get that close is our grooming clique.

So next Dunbar took that number of the average ape clique and the average human clique and compared their size. Then he looked at the difference in size between an ape brain (a grapefruit), and our human brains (a honeydew melon). And guess what—the difference was the same. Our social group was bigger in proportion to the bigger size of our brain. From that moment on the upper limit of a human social group has been known as Dunbar's Number. What is the number? It's 150 (in fact it was 148, but he rounded it up, which I find likeably casual of him).

To anthropologists, 150 seemed close enough to 120 for the difference not really to matter. And that sounds like a worrying leap for our theory about cell phones. After all, 30 extra names is a lot to account for on anyone's contact list. But closer inspection of Dunbar's definition of this social group reveals the badly needed loophole. His circle of 150 contacts includes old buddies we've lost touch with but could easily pick up with again because we still have all that valuable data. The social bond is strong, just dormant. In other words, we remember them, but we don't have their phone numbers!

So if you deduct 30 to cover all those we've lost touch with, the magic 120 lives on. And we now understand why it's important to keep clearing out the phone memory, too. More than 120 means brain strain. It just feels wrong. The phone could store far more, but what's the point? We'd never call them, and we know it. They just don't belong.

THE FACEBOOK PROOF

The cell phone is a constant companion, and we prefer it to mirror the capacity of our brains, not to add to it like some kind of plug-in hard drive. But what about online networking sites like Facebook? Dunbar predicted they could be the end of his magic number. These sites are all about acquiring "friends" who can send their profile with a click, allowing us to boost our circle of friends exponentially, without unlimited RAM.

Well in early 2009, *The Economist* magazine asked Facebook to crunch some numbers and tell them on average how many "friends" each Facebook user has. And Facebook came up with an answer that seems too good to be true. It was 120. This is all very reassuring for anyone who likes to think that friendship is about nothing more than data storage. Despite the runaway potential of new technology, the primate brain holds sway.

THINGS TO DO IN STARBUCKS

Use your Starbucks state of mind to reconnect with a more resourceful past.

The low lighting, the comfy seats, and those subtle shades of brown are working overtime to make you feel at home and buy another latte. And it's effective, you have to admit. Of course, you're right not to be taken in by the folksy logo and the green aprons; there's nothing homespun about Starbucks at all. But what fascinates me is that the story being sold here is so seductive. It's all about nostalgia, wafting us on a cloud of butterscotch froth back to a time when life was simple, time was plentiful, and coffee cost much less than $4 a hit. It's artfully done, and it took millions of dollars of venture capital to pull it off, so you may as well make good use of it.

STIRRER STAR RACE

Time: ten minutes

The sticks that are used to stir coffee may look like lollipop sticks, but they have a critical difference: extra flexibility. This is what makes it possible to construct the star (see opposite page), all held together with nothing but friction. If making Christmas decorations isn't your thing, you can always reinvent them as Kung Fu death stars.

Have a race to see who can make one first, starting with the simplest five-stick model.

Other stirrer art projects could include: wicker man, moon lander, stick insect.

This is what you should end up with:

LATTE LINGO BINGO

For two players or more.

Here's a sample bingo card. I'm sure you can work it out for yourself from here.

SKINNY	SHOT	VENTI	CHAI
LATTE	GRANDE	CAPPUCCINO	VERY BERRY

FROTHY PERSONALITIES PREDICTOR

At busy times this works especially well. You need a seat near the service area. The aim is to predict what drink each person in the line is going to buy, and it's uncanny how easy it is to get this right. A good variation of the game is to take turns guessing the drink and the size of cup of each order. An online application called Starbucks Oracle gives each Starbucks drink a corresponding personality type. Look it up if you must. In this game you just use your instinctive knowledge of these fairly obvious associations. Sometimes you can look at someone, and you just know they're a skinny decaf frappuccino.

THREE THINGS YOU DIDN'T KNOW ABOUT STARBUCKS

THERE IS A SMALL SIZE

They don't advertise it on the menu, but it's on the pricing structure—and the staff all know about it. Ask for a "short" (of course they wouldn't call it "small"). The actual size (# of ounces) is a third smaller than the next smallest ("tall"), but with the same single shot. Cappuccino connoisseurs will recognize immediately that this is much closer to the Italian way of making the drink—maximum coffee, minimum froth.

THE FOAM HAT TRICK

On a cold day ask for extra foam on top of your coffee. It keeps it warm, like a woolly hat.

"THAT'S GROSS, DUDE"

Starbucks baristas on a staff blog compare notes on their most disgusting drink orders. Last time I looked, the winner was something called a "triple grande pomegranate fruit juice frappuccino."

8.
THE FUTURE

Urban bushcraft kicks against the idea that progress has to be one way. If the clock went into reverse, just imagine what you'd discover. Life would be one long relearning curve. At the start you'd find out how we really did manage without cell phones, and by the end you'd know how to build your own pyramid.

A lot of what we call bushcraft, urban or otherwise, comes from this resourceful past. In compiling this book, it's been my pleasure to watch some fairly rustic survival skills take off their muddy boots and help out around the modern home, or come blundering into town and adapt to the modern city.

But the urban bushman has another greater source of knowledge, and we're only just beginning to tap into its riches. I'm talking about the wisdom of the great urban tribesmen. I call it urban lore, and it comes from those special people in our cities who are supremely adapted to their habitat.

It's people like taxi drivers, real estate agents, and supermarket security guards. It's the long-distance truck driver with an instinct for finding the best rest stop. And it's the corner bakery owner who has developed the ability to tell a genuine shopper from a chocolate thief or pie snatcher, not to mention the instinct for knowing just how many schoolchildren to allow in the bakery at one time. Like the bushmen of the Kalahari, they'd be pretty useless anywhere else, but on their home patch they're unbeatable. The true urban bushman mingles with these master practitioners, studies their behavior, and considers it an honor to preserve their skills for future generations.

I once had the honor of spending several days making paper darts with a man descended from a long line of office stationery suppliers. His ability to select on sight the ideal weight of paper for any dart was staggering. I was humbled as he effortlessly adapted his construction technique to suit the paper available; his choice

changed with the purpose of each dart, from long-distance glider to stunt plane. This was urban lore at work.

These ancient oral traditions are passed down from father to son in wisdom encoded into their culture. It's the urban bushman's duty to preserve as many of these skills and secrets as he can, to ensure a brighter future. We either use it or lose it.

EPILOGUE

After this book was published in Britain, I got asked to speak at a seminar about it. The attendees were interested in ingenuity and its meaning today. It was fun, and people liked some of these stories. As I said at the start, everyone loves the idea of finding a neat way to unravel the complications of modern life. The one about the broken windshield wipers and how my dad fixed them with string went over really well. I saw one guy beaming at me from the back and took it as confirmation of just that.

Later over sandwiches and soda, he came up and said he wanted to tell me a story but had to go give a lecture, so he'd e-mail me. His name was Kevin. A few weeks later, his e-mail arrived. And the story he sent was this.

The windshield wiper thing happened to him, too. Except it wasn't his dad who'd fixed them, it was Kevin himself. The story was identical with a few key details changed. Instead of family, he was traveling with friends. And instead of string (which he didn't have), he used the laces (from his Doc Marten boots). The laces seemed to me like an advance on string in terms of ingenuity, but I was relieved to find out it was a bit less practical. The shorter length of the laces meant he and his friend pulling the strings needed to stretch their arms out of the window into the rain.

Anyhow, no sooner had I overcome my competitive urge over who owned the whole windshield wiper thing, Then I found out we both did. Kevin's story has an ending that makes him more than welcome in the brotherhood of string, and, forever grateful he got in touch.

One of the passengers was a young woman he hardly knew. But she was so impressed by his brilliance with his bootlaces, she accepted first a ride home, then a doorstep kiss. And now, years later, she and Kevin are the happy parents of three kids, and they happily retell their windshield wiper anecdote as often as they can.

So there it is. Living proof of how simple stuff like this turns an ordinary day into a life-changing adventure. How about that, Dad?